The Little ROAD TRIP Handbook

by Erin McHugh

STERLING

New York / London
www.sterlingpublishing.com

DEDICATION

To the three greatest Road Trip friends anyone could ever have—
my Stillman girls: Julie Stillman, Ann Stillman O'Leary, and Martha
Stillman Otis.

STERLING and the distinctive Sterling logo are registered trademarks of
Sterling Publishing Co., Inc.

Library of Congress Cataloging-in-Publication Data

McHugh, Erin.
  The little road trip handbook / Erin McHugh.
      p. cm.
  ISBN 978-1-4027-3161-7
  1. Automobile travel—United States—Guidebooks. 2. Automobile driving—United
States—Guidebooks. 3. United States—Guidebooks. I. Title.
  GV1021.M244 2009
  917.304'931—dc22

                                                                    2008034697

10 9 8 7 6 5 4 3 2 1

Published by Sterling Publishing Co., Inc.
387 Park Avenue South, New York, NY 10016
© 2009 by Erin McHugh
Illustrations © 2009 by John Kachik
Distributed in Canada by Sterling Publishing
c/o Canadian Manda Group, 165 Dufferin Street
Toronto, Ontario, Canada M6K 3H6
Distributed in the United Kingdom by GMC Distribution Services
Castle Place, 166 High Street, Lewes, East Sussex, England BN7 1XU
Distributed in Australia by Capricorn Link (Australia) Pty. Ltd.
P.O. Box 704, Windsor, NSW 2756, Australia

Book Design: Rachel Maloney
Illustrations: John Kachik
Photo credits: All photos courtesy Shutterstock Images with the following exceptions:
Wikimedia pages 16, 68, 112, 131, 162; Photos.com pages 117, 118 top image; Library
of Congress pages 125, 130.

Sterling ISBN 978-1-4027-3161-7

For information about custom editions, special sales, premium and
corporate purchases, please contact Sterling Special Sales
Department at 800-805-5489 or specialsales@sterlingpublishing.com.

CONTENTS

INTRODUCTION

"When you come to a fork in the road, take it!"
—YOGI BERRA

If these words resonate with you, then you are ready for this gonzo guide to The Road Trip—The Road Trip as an attitudinal art form, that is.

Why? Because you must be the type that either still thrives on—or longs to re-capture—the compulsive, unfettered feeling of just plain being alive that comes with a real what-the-hell-let's-go-for-it Road Trip adventure.

It's addictive; it's a rush. I speak of Guerrilla Tripping, where you start with absolutely nothing except the bare essentials—gas money, beer, a car that's not necessarily fancy, but one with panache and one you can count on when the chips are down and the rain is pelting.

I grew up in the seafaring town of New Bedford, Massachusetts, with my back to the ocean and my face to the teeming cities of the Northeast. And perhaps—no definitely—that's why I truly appreciate the wide open spaces that unfurl before you on a full-tilt Road Trip. Everything was "Out West" to me until I met Road

Tripping, and once we became acquainted, there was no turning back.

The Road Trip urge usually begins with a whiff: the earthy smell of a February thaw or the scent of the salt sea. It's a tease, a promise of warm weather and all-out adventure to come. It's when the song on continuous loop in your head is either "School's Out" or "California Dreamin'" and the download won't stop; when your fingers twitch in eager anticipation longing to grip the wheel once again; and when your face is locked in the rictus smile of pure joy, for no reason at all. You know there's no point in trying to deny this siren call: you have got to roll.

" Strap your hands cross my engines. "
—BRUCE SPRINGSTEEN

Perhaps you're planning a Road Trip for the first time, or for the first time in a long time. And, I mean, a really long time. You've been living a safe life measured by friends and lovers, waiting in restaurants, bosses and their deadlines, or expectant threesomes at the first tee. Think back to the person you used to be when Friday nights weren't about candy-sweet frozen margaritas and something naughty on a DVD. Remember when you had just enough crumpled-up folding money for a case of beer and vague directions to some wild party in another state and you got in the car and DROVE? You didn't think about it, plan for it, or get permission: you just hit the road.

I know it's hard to leave your safe life behind, even for just a week. And sure, some of your running buddies might be making it big in that life of theirs. One runs his own hedge fund, makes a gazillion dollars, drinks Chateau Petrus like it was Gatorade—*and* still manages to avoid prosecution. And, yeah, others might enjoy successful careers as gold-digging supermodels or politicians who regularly appear on *The Colbert Report*, but to what end? Perhaps you're even one of "those" people. Except, you ask yourself "how long can anybody dine out on a life like *that*?" And then you think of the open road with no destination and no time schedule, which makes you instantly relax, every time.

The Little Road Trip Handbook will help you get back behind the wheel. Remember that place? It's where by right you belong. The American Road Trip isn't just a pastime it's a birthright, a necessity, a rite of passage, and, even in the teeth of spiraling fuel costs, it's a way of life. Can any American feel complete if he hasn't taken at least one cross-country Road Trip? It doesn't seem possible. We Americans have been fulfilling our manifest destiny ever since we arrived on these shores. Why, we rode west in covered wagons for heaven's sake, and didn't the entire nation hear Horace Greeley tell that young man to go west? OK, I grant you, Greeley may have been referring to New Jersey at the time, but the truth remains that travel across America—from sea to shining sea—has always been how we've gotten our heads cleared and where we sought solutions to our collective problems. Travel is how we renew our souls and celebrate our freedom. And you thought it was just a drive?

From behind the wheel of our cars we see the USA and find ourselves. We travel beyond our familiar borders and lose ourselves to the greater collective. Like the dharma bums we think we are, we seek the truth within. It's where we're tested and set loose, where we discover. A Road Trip can either prove our friendships or teach us the value of going it alone. Besides, if we didn't Road Trip we'd never know how truly sweet it is to come home sweet home.

Of course, there's just about nothing more fun than an evening on the road: car parked, bed secured, a whole town to discover by moon or streetlight, and the promise of local food and cheap drink safely nearby.

THE LITTLE ROAD TRIP HANDBOOK encourages you to rethink your life. You'll rediscover how to make memories you can never tell your grandchildren, at least until you reach the point when you're so old that anything goes—and usually does.

Every time you choose to fly *over* rather than drive *through* these United States, you are robbing your body and soul of a

chance to see America on your own terms, on your own schedule, and at your own pace. C'mon! See your country as it was meant to be seen, how it was *designed* to be explored. Forget about long lines, homeland security, and high-priced tickets. Why should you race to keep yourself on schedule when you know the plane will take off at least an hour late? Slow down, take your time, be one with your forefathers—a link in the unbroken chain of serious Trippers.

Today, America is Road Trip Heaven, and we often take our freedom of flight for granted. Although America was founded by Trippers, life on the road hasn't always been so easy going. Back in 1903, the automobile was just coming into its own, with only about one hundred and fifty miles of paved roads throughout the entire United States. But lack of roads didn't stop the intrepid Dr. Horatio Nelson Jackson from betting that he could drive his new-fangled horseless carriage clear across the United States. It was a $50 bet, no less, which was quite a hefty wager back in the days when men were men and a dollar was a big load of cash. And his horseless carriage was more like a twenty-horsepower glorified wagon, which he loaded up with a mechanic named Sewall Crocker and a bulldog named Bud. OK maybe it's not what you'd call a sweet ride, but it was historic. Horatio Nelson Jackson invented the American Road Trip the day he set off in his Winton automobile, and we've never looked back.

Soon, it seems, everyone was buying automobiles, and Americans started traveling further and further from home more often, frequently just for fun. There were still very few highways, let alone accommodations, so early drivers relied on hotels and campsites for overnight stays, and the choice depended on whether they landed in a city or in a more remote location. That is until 1925 when Arthur Heineman built a little hideaway—a kind of hotel on the highway—in San Luis Obispo, California, which is halfway between San Francisco and Los Angeles. He named his little hideaway the Milestone Motor Hotel, but when he went to install the sign, he decided to combine Motor and Hotel, adding a hyphen, he came up with MOTEL. Arthur's new sign read, "The Milestone Mo-Tel," and, once again, Road Trip history was made. Heineman's new motel provided customers with a two-room bungalow, garage, an outdoor swimming pool, and picnic tables. Heaven at just $1.25 per night, and it sure beat camping.

Clearly, traffic was picking up, and in 1926 the federal government commissioned the building of Route 66. It was the first of many national highways and the longest in North America. So long, in fact, that John Steinbeck dubbed it "The Mother Road," in his novel, *The Grapes of Wrath*. This long and often lonesome highway stretched for 2,448 miles and ran through eight states—Illinois, Missouri, Kansas, Oklahoma, Texas, New Mexico, Arizona, and California The American public, long frustrated by the lack of real roads on which to drive their new automobiles, took to Route 66 like ducks to water, and almost overnight "The Mother Road" became an icon of American life. In fact Route 66 was so well known that it spawned an eponymous popular TV show, a classic rock and roll song, and Winona Judd's first name. What? Yes, it's true. Naomi chose the name because it was one of the towns mentioned in the song. (Perhaps she, too, got her kicks on Route 66!)

Sadly, the engineering miracle known as the U.S. Interstate System began to replace the old national highway system during the Eisenhower years, signaling the doom of Route 66. While 85 percent of it is still drivable today, it no longer appears on most road maps or atlases. If you want to know where to find it, you'll have to turn to the Internet. And remember to print the directions and take them with you! It's still a drive worth taking, and it's the King of the Roads for the complete Road Tripper.

We've come along way since then, and the concept of Road Tripping has become the stuff of high and low American culture, legend, and lore. It's celebrated in books, songs, and movies and has spawned those serious—and now legendary—Trippers, the Beats: William Burroughs, Allen Ginsberg, and the Merry Prankster driver of the infamous psychedelic bus, Ken Kesey.

During the 1950s, Kesey was the road pal of Jack Kerouac, the godfather of Road Tripping and author of the classic novel, *On the Road*, which did as much to ignite Road Trip fever in the 1960s as Route 66 had in the 1920s. Suddenly, *everybody* wanted to be on the road again. And this new wave of Road Trip fever brought us some excellent Road Trip movies: *Easy Rider*, *Bonnie & Clyde*, *Natural Born Killers*, *Thelma and Louise*, and more. And what's one of the very best Road Trip movies ever made without a single car in the entire film? *The Wizard of Oz*, of course! Although Dorothy and the gang travel by means of twister, foot, and hot air balloon, the film perfectly captures the Road Trip dream: somewhere over the rainbow, there's a golden highway leading us through a brave and magical world filled with new friends, adventure, danger, discovery, and, best of all, the joy of returning home and crawling back into your own bed. (Often with a metaphoric bump on the head, but what the hell.)

> **"** *Come, and trip it, as you go,*
> *On the light fantastic toe.* **"**
> — JOHN MILTON

Part One

PRE-IGNITION CHECK

All Revved Up and Nowhere to Go: Seven Classic Road Trips

There's a certain type of Road Trip you take for no reason whatsoever, except to heed the call of the highway, whose beckoning grows louder each day it's ignored, reaching its crescendo only when, restless and reckless, you can take it no more. With a little dharma, that'll be the moment when you, along with a friend or two, just happen to have a little bit of time on your hands.

So what kind of Road Trip do you take? They used to say, "See America first," and in order to do so, there are seven extra-special Road Trips scattered throughout this book. You'll find very different and equally extraordinary slices of American roadways—enough to wet your whistle and make you long to put the top down on that big old convertible.

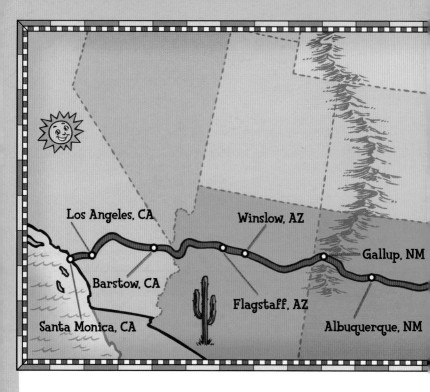

CLASSIC ROAD TRIP #1—ROUTE 66

John Steinbeck first called it "The Mother Road" in *The Grapes of Wrath*, and he was right: Route 66 is owed the reverence, respect, and idolatry normally reserved for one's own Mom.

Commissioned in 1926, this long—and sometimes lonesome—highway covered 2,448 miles through eight states: Illinois, Missouri, Kansas, Oklahoma, Texas, New Mexico, Arizona, and California. It crosses three time zones (which is great for the inveterate Road

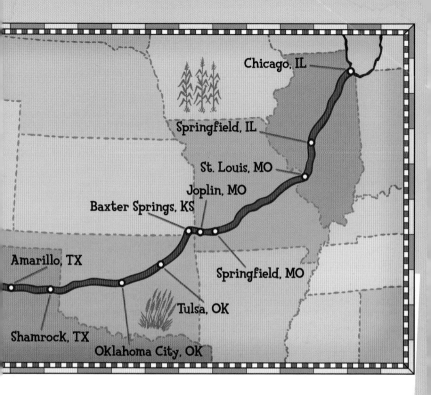

Tripper, especially if you travel east to west), starting in Chicago and ending in Santa Monica. But in the 1960s, Route 66 took a back seat to the new superhighways, and in 1984, it was decommissioned and the last stretch disappeared off the records.

However, "The Main Street of America" has become such a part of our history that many books and websites are available to aid the Road Tripper in bringing back the good old days. (Try www.historic66.com, www.national66.com, and www.route66.com for starters.) In those times, we simply weren't in as much of a hurry to get there—wherever *there* was.

CHAPTER 1

IT'S ALL ABOUT THE CAR

Or, All the Basics a Driver Needs to Know to Get
Going—and Stay on the Road

The journey of a thousand miles begins with a single step, and these are the steps you'll need to take to ensure a successful Trip. I know, a Road Trip is supposed to be spontaneous, but you're old enough to know by now that sometimes flat out, headlong spontaneity is rewarded with heavy fines, jail time, or a trip to the ER. So please listen up, every one of these is an absolute necessity for hitting the road. Don't make me say I told you so.

Make Sure You Have and Are Familiar with Your Car Manual

Live and learn. A couple of times I've been in the unfortunate position of having something go wrong with the car on a Road Trip. I've reached into the glove compartment only to find . . . a bunch of napkins from McDonald's. No sign of the manual that came with the car at all. Making sure your car's owner's manual is in the glove compartment should always be Item #1 on your pre-Trip checklist. First, check to see that it's in the glove compartment, and then check to make sure that it matches the make, model, and year of the car you're planning to drive. You should go no further in your Trip planning if you haven't checked both.

If you've lost your manual, or if your "pre-owned vehicle" didn't come with one, chances are good you can download one online or get one from your nearest dealer.

Once you locate the correct owner's manual, make sure you understand the purpose of every dial, gauge, and meter on your dashboard. Some of them, such as the tachometer, are pretty much just for show, unless you've got a NASCAR thing going on, but when those mysterious little icons with unrecognizable pictures start blinking on and off, you really want to know whether it means "get some gas soon, dude," or "your engine is in serious trouble."

Get Yourself a AAA Card

Some late-model marques provide several years of complementary roadside service as part of your car's warranty package. This will protect you from breakdowns, flats, and inadvertent lock-outs throughout the country.

ALASKA
is said to have a great view of Russia

However, if the car you're driving doesn't come with such a program, consider the AAA. The cost for membership in the American Automobile Association remains afford-able and accessible, and if you find you need to use their services only once a year, you'll discover joining is worth every penny and more. Just one flat tire on a rainy night or a single time having to be towed out of a ditch or snow bank will have you patting your-self on the back. There are also some incredible membership bene-fits, like 30 percent off eyewear at a top-notch national chain.

At this writing, minimum membership costs around $55 per year for the primary member of a household (the first to join), plus $10 initiation fee. Renewals are around $47. Associate members—those living in the same household—are $10 to $20 each. However, rates vary across the country; there are a number of membership levels that will affect the costs and services offered. Please check with your local office.

For $65, it's the best insurance you can get. When bad things happen, AAA will show up. If only you could find a relationship like that.

A Few of the Benefits AAA Provides

- **Emergency "First Aid":** Free delivery of a limited amount of fuel; enough to enable the member to reach the nearest service station.

- **Towing:** Up to 100 miles of free towing from the point of disablement.

- **Maps and TripTiks®:** Driving directions for any Trip you're planning.

- **Enhanced Trip Delay Coverage**: When you're more than 100 miles from home and your car becomes disabled, you may be reimbursed to cover reasonable expenses.

- **AAA Travel Emergency Hotline (800) 692-2234:** Provides emergency medical transportation and assistance, medical consulting and monitoring, travel document and ticket replacement assistance, legal assistance, emergency cash transfer, and more.

" *The untended Kosmos my abode,*
I pass, a willful stranger;
My mistress still the open road
And the bright eyes of danger. "
— ROBERT LOUIS STEVENSON

Do a Complete Pre-Trip Car Check

Before you turn the key and head out on the open highway—and we don't mean ten minutes before you're ready to roll—you need to check all of the following: gas (you're never lost with a full tank of gas), oil, wiper fluid, wiper blades, coolant, tires (make sure your spare is there and filled with air), and brakes, and don't forget the lights—head and tail lamps.

OK, you passed your state inspection, but that was eleven months ago. Your pre-flight car check should include a visual inspection of all headlights, fog lights, tail lights, side/front/rear directional lights, and the brake lights. Did you find a problem with one of your lights? See your trusty local fix-it guy, a.k.a., your mechanic. In days of yore, all you needed was a screwdriver, but with today's hi-tech sealed beams and high-zoom xenon jobbies, repairing your own lights has become a thing of the past unless

ALABAMA *hosted the first Mardi Gras in the Western world in Mobile Bay in 1703.*

you're one of those do-it-yourselfers on Saturday afternoon cable. Having a busted light is just what a cop trying to make his quota of tickets is looking for. It's a really easy way to get stopped—and it's a hazard, too. Check all of your lights carefully before you head out on the open road.

Now to get you truly road-ready—and don't freak your freak—here are some basic chores that you may never have tackled, but they're all easy to do and helpful to know. Remember, with any luck, you'll be putting miles upon miles of blacktop between your car and filling stations or repair shops. A little on-the-road maintenance can go a long way toward making your Trip more fun. And there are just some things a Tripper has to do for him/herself.

Check and Fill Your Tires

If you're suspicious that a tire seems low while you're on the road, you can check it yourself with a tire gauge. It's small so you can pop it right in your glove compartment (right next to this book!) and costs less than $10. Any store with an auto parts section will have one. Just unscrew the valve cap on the tire in question and press the gauge onto the valve. The little meter on the top will tell you the tire's pressure.

If you've just been driving, wait until the tires have cooled to the touch—the reading will be more accurate.

Tire pressure is measured in PSI (pounds per square inch). Check your owner's manual (see, I told you you'd need it) for the correct tire pressure for your car and driving conditions. Why? Because if you intend to drive fast or carry a heavy load, your tires will perform better with higher tire pressure (PSI). Your manual also will tell you whether or not the PSI for front and rear tires is the same. If you're car isn't new, and the tires aren't original, you'll want to learn how to read the information on the tire itself. I know, it sounds like too much already, but, trust me, once you figure it out (ask your mechanic for help), you'll never run low again.

Driving with your tires properly inflated will reduce your fuel consumption, will improve the quality of your ride, and is the only safe way to cruise. In fact, experts say that getting the tire pressure right can save you nearly ten cents a gallon, which is a lot of money when you're gobbling up miles and miles of highway. So make sure that every time you stop for gas you check your tire pressure too; it only takes a minute.

Change a Tire

Oh yes, you can. Even if you've never seen the inside of a gym, you can master this task; it's not as hard as it looks. Between the lug-loosening thing and jacking the car off the road, everyone gets a little scared, but neither function is about upper-body strength. Never was. It's all about the aerosol lubricant, a magic fix-it elixir in a can, and safe, proper use of the car's jack.

Lug nuts first: spray some aerosol lubricant liberally on all the lug nuts of the flat tire (yeah, all of them.) Tap them with your lug wrench—you know, the one you said was in your trunk next to your spare tire. Wait a minute. Spray again. Tap again. Apply your lug wrench to the nuts and loosen—but do not remove—them. If all else fails, you can actually step on the lug wrench while it's on the tire—even give a little hop if it's still tight—and that should solve the loosening problem (works for me every time.) Once the lugs are loose, it's time to jack the car up in order to replace the flat tire with your spare.

Every car has an *exact* place where you need to place the jack, and this info is—you guessed it—in your owner's manual. Read it carefully, and place the jack properly.

Of course, you can always call the AAA, but if your Road Trip brings you far afield from society's conveniences (like towns and gas stations), the wait will cost you many pleasurable hours. Think it over. Sometimes doing it yourself is still the best plan.

Check and Add Oil

Oil is like gas and coolant. You really need it if you want to take a Road Trip of any duration. And you should check it whenever you gas up. Check your manual again; it will tell you where the dipstick is under your hood. The dipstick tells you the oil level of your car. Shut off the engine. Remove the dipstick. Wipe it clean. Reinsert the dipstick. Remove it once again, and now check the oil level. It should lie between "LOW" and "FULL" on the etched lines of the dipstick. Your owner's manual shows where to add the oil (no, it's not down the teensy dipstick hole) as well as the type and amount of oil you'll need. And remember: do not overfill. Confused? A full-service gas station (i.e., one with a garage and employees) will gladly check and add oil for you. Sadly, the majority of places that sell gasoline these days only employ workers

ARIZONA *has the most land devoted to Indian reservations; the Navajo Nation covers 27,000 square miles.*

to mind the mini-mart register; they don't go outside. Gas or beef jerky—it's all the same to them. So it's a good idea to get the whole changing oil thing figured out before you go.

Check and Add Coolant

If the coolant gets too low, your engine will overheat, and that, if left unchecked for too long, will destroy your car. Not good. So check the coolant in your radiator before you go, and make sure you check it each time you stop for gas.

The coolant level should be between the "LOW" and "FULL" marks on the clear coolant overflow container under the hood. If it's low, top it up with radiator coolant—a premixed cocktail that's 50 percent water and 50 percent coolant or antifreeze. They sell it by the jug at gasoline service stations and in auto parts stores. But only fill the radiator after the engine is cool (wait at least a few minutes after the car has been turned off) and add enough coolant so that the gauge reaches the "FULL" mark.

Never open the radiator when the engine is hot or the coolant will overflow the tank. That's never!

Add Windshield Wiper Fluid

Wiper fluid is stored in a plastic holding tank under the hood of your car. The fluid itself is often blue liquid, and you can see it—or what's left of it—in its semi-transparent plastic container. Wiper fluid is cheap—under $2 for a big plastic jug—so keep a jug in the trunk of your car, always. Keeping your windshield clean is one of the easiest ways to prevent accidents, and adding wiper fluid couldn't be easier.

ARKANSAS *has the only diamond mine in the world which is open to the public, in Murfreesboro.*

Change Windshield Wiper Blades

You can buy wiper blades for most popular car models at any auto supply store or good gasoline service station. Change both front wiper blades as well as the one for the back window if your car has one. The process can be a little tricky, but the new package will provide instructions, and your car owner's manual will be helpful, too. Of course, your new friend at the service station can fix them for you.

Change Fuses

How do you know you've burned out a fuse? Simple: something will suddenly stop working, like your lights. Before that happens to you, learn where your fuse box is, and familiarize yourself with its layout. The fuse box is easy to spot and is usually inside a pop-out panel under the dashboard; your owner's manual will pinpoint its exact location. The manual will also show which fuse does what job. Of course, if a fuse has already burned out, it will be easy enough to spot. Just pull the one that look's burned out (often you'll find the glass has turned black) and replace it. Extra fuses should be provided in the fuse box, but check before setting off on your Trip. If there aren't extras, buy some. Consider it cheap insurance.

Jump-Start a Dead Battery

I mean, what are the chances that someone's going to happen along with a set of jumper cables just moments after you discover your battery's dead? It is possible that you may have just popped into a convenient roadhouse to slake your thirst, accidentally leaving your headlights on in your giddy excitement, and that the tavern is full of friendly locals with monster trucks full of all the best tools, such as jumper cables. But we all know that a synergistic convergence such as this is not something we can rely on. It's time you learn how to charge up your battery so that you can get on your way.

First, loosen the purse strings a little, and go buy some decent jumper cables; they're under $50. Then start rehearsing your most fetching smile: even with your own cables you're going to need someone willing to help you out. Someone who has a car that's in working order, too. But I'm sure you have your ways, and frankly, I don't want to know about them. Even if your car's battery is dead, getting it started again with good jumper cables is easy. But some people can never remember the right order in which to do things or what color clamp goes where. So here we go: learn and remember.

How to Jump-Start Your Car

1. Turn off the booster car. (Yours, as we know, is already off.)
2. Clamp one end of the *red* jumper cable to the *positive* end (+) of the dead battery.
3. Clamp the other *red* end to the *positive* end (+) of the booster car battery.
4. Clamp the *black* jumper cable to the booster battery's *negative* (–) terminal.
5. Clamp the other end of the *black* cable to *any solid metal (non-painted) part on the car's dead engine*; this is called a ground. (If you see a spark, that's normal. Don't flip.)
6. Turn on the booster car, and give it a little gas.
7. Turn on the dead car.
8. Now, disconnect the cables in *reverse* order.

You're back on the road.

Just remember a couple of things: the two cars should not be touching, and make sure that everything in both cars is turned off: radios, HVAC systems, fans, cell phones unplugged, etc. If there is any sign of a crack in the battery case of the dead car, don't attempt to jump start it. The battery could explode. If you see a crack in the battery's casing, you'll need to buy a new battery. Incidentally, unless your car's battery is truly dead—as in you need to buy a new one—the engine's alternator will automatically recharge your "dead" battery as the motor runs.

Familiarize Yourself with Every Nuance of Your Sound System

Frankly, this should have come first. You have no business putting your key in the ignition without having your musical house in order. Study your car's sound system carefully, and make sure that it is in perfect working order (that includes speakers without cracks) and that you know how to use it.

NORTH CAROLINA *was home to the first miniature golf course in Pinehurst, called Thistle Dhu ("This'll Do").*

Learn How to Read a Map

Sheesh! Did I really have to say that?

" Badness you can get easily, in quantity: the road is smooth, and it lies close by. "

— HESIOD

Chapter 2

WHAT ARE YOU PACKING?

Or, the Junk in Your Trunk (and in Your Wallet)

Road Trip Checklist

Here is a list of what you absolutely, positively *must* take with you (or should at least think about.) Some of what is on this list we've already discussed in Chapter 1. If you want to load in a lot of other stuff like clothes, that's your business. I'm just here to tell you what you need—for real.

✓ Driver's License

Not just yours—check that the whole team has his or hers, and I don't mean the old, expired ones, either. Every driver or potential driver must have a current, legitimate driver's license. Even if you have a fellow Road Tripper who

doesn't intend on ever driving, plans can always change, often unexpectedly. If they can drive and have a license, they must have it with them, and it must be legit. If they can't and don't, why are they part of your team? Besides, lots of clubs make you present a valid I.D. even if you do look like Grandma Moses.

✓ Car Registration and Insurance Info Card

Always keep your insurance card (the current one!) in the glove compartment. It's the universal spot. Keep your registration in your wallet, next to your license. You do have your license, don't you? Don't even think about leaving the driveway without these three documents; that's *all* three.

✓ Passport

As of December 31, 2006, U.S. laws became much more stringent about crossing the borders. You may no longer reenter the United States from Canada or Mexico with just a birth certificate: you need a passport. I think there's plenty of road to explore right here in the U S of A, but if you are truly open to adventure, you may need a passport. Your best place to start is to call the State Department National Passport Information Center's toll-free number 1-877-487-2778. Their website (where you can also download an application) gives you lots of information on passports. You'll find that, for a fee, you can get around the usual six-week wait and get your passport pronto. The last thing you want to happen is to be left at the border while everyone else pops off for a big blow out in Tijuana!

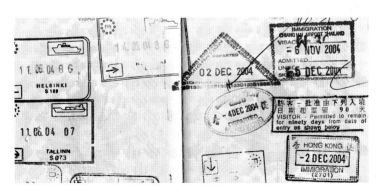

Speedy Passport Info

U.S. Department of State's Bureau of Consular Affairs
Office of Passport Services/Customer Service
www.travel.state.gov
(202) 647-4000 (Department of State)

Passport Expedition Services

Passports and Visas.com
www.passportsandvisas.com
(800) 860-8610
(ranked #1 by U.S. Passport Service Guide, a third-party
   review service)

U.S. Passport Service Guide
www.us-passport-service-guide.com

√ Cell Phone, Cell Phone Car Charger, Hands-Free Kit

Several states have made hands-free talking the law, with more states to come. It's ticket time if you are caught driving while holding your mobile phone. Think Bluetooth, baby. It's convenient and, let's face it, safer. And wouldn't it be a bitch if, after all these years, *that's* what got you pulled over? Spend the bucks, and have one on hand. And don't forget your cell phone charger, either.

✓ Full Tank of Gas

A full tank of gas, especially on a budget Trip, is the most important thing to start out with. Don't get cheap with gasoline along the road, either; always keep your tank full. If you see a station alongside the highway and your fuel gauge is less than half full, stop to fuel up. Don't forget: you're never lost with a full tank of gas.

> *Note:* Another reason not to let the tank drain down to nearly empty: sediment from the bottom of the tank is more likely to mix with the gasoline and clog your fuel lines. Translation: your engine dies a slow and tragic death, leaving you stranded somewhere west of Laramie.

✓ Water

Unopened bottles of water can literally be a lifesaver. Take several large bottles each for you and your Trip Mates. After twenty minutes in bumper-to-bumper traffic outside Phoenix in August, you'll know why it's just about a life-and-death necessity.

It's also a good idea to have a gallon container of water for the radiator in your trunk at all times (in addition to coolant) to prevent overheating. Need I say, especially when traveling in hot weather or whenever you're within sight of a desert?

> " *Afoot and light-hearted I take to the open road,*
> *Healthy, free, the road before me,*
> *The long brown path before me before me leading*
> *wherever I choose.* "
>
> —WALT WHITMAN

Need a Cup to Runneth Over?

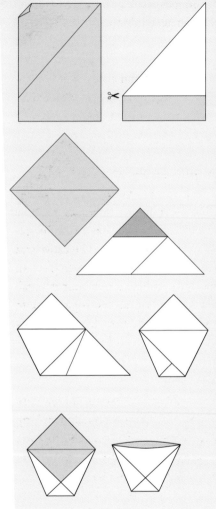

Procure a piece of paper— basic 8$\frac{1}{2}$ by 11 is good for a final cup size, though any size will do in a pinch.

Now you have to make a triangle, so take the upper left-hand corner and fold it over to meet the right-hand side of the page. (The top edge of the sheet of paper now lines up along the right edge.)

Fold up remaining portion, tear off, and discard. Turn the long side of the triangle toward your.

Fold left corner to intersect halfway up right side of the triangle and crease crisply. Repeat by folding the right-hand corner to the left side of the triangle. Fold top flaps down and pull open. There's your cup! Bottoms up!

√ Oil

Your owner's manual will tell you what type of oil your car likes. Buy a quart of good quality oil, and keep it in the car.

√ Radiator Coolant

Get a gallon of premixed radiator coolant and check your coolant level along with your oil and tire pressure often on the road, before you start out in the morning. Why? 'Cause you ain't going nowhere, no-how, if your engine overheats.

√ Spare Tire (Tire-Changing Tools and Gauge)

Duh. But you absolutely positively have to make sure it's there—and *properly inflated*—before you leave home. It wouldn't be the first time someone forgot to pick up the old flat from the gas station. And more importantly, make really sure the tire gauge and other tire-changing stuff, such as the jack and lug wrench are in there. (If you don't know what it looks like, check your manual. Better yet, open up your trunk, throw out all the soggy junk in there, and inspect your spare tire and all the tire-changing equipment, including the jack.)

√ WD-40

Two cans of the aerosol version should be packed onboard for every Road Trip. Its magic aerosol powers of lubrication help you keep all locks operating and can unfreeze rusted wheel nuts allowing you to change that blown tire when you're fifty miles east of Nowheresville. And, you don't want to be there, trust me.

✓ Duct Tape

I consider this, along with WD-40 to be an essential tool in the Road Tripper's must-have kit. In a pinch, duct tape can be used to fix bumpers, reattach mufflers, and stifle overly chatty passengers. Comes in high-fashion colors, too!

✓ Jumper Cables

This bears repeating: don't get the cheapest ones. And, again: DON'T GET THE CHEAPEST ONES!!! Jumper cables are affordable insurance against getting stranded because of a dopey, dead battery. Cheap ones pull apart, don't carry enough juice, and can be too short to help. We've been there. And it was really cold out.

✓ Windshield Wiper Fluid

Because it's kind of hard to drive when you can't see where the blankety-blank you're going. It's dangerous, too.

✓ Extra Car Fuses

A small thing, but you can avoid a real hassle if one blows.

✓ Windshield Scraper

This is a must for those winter flings, or late spring and early autumn, or if you're traveling in the mountains, or wherever weather changes rapidly: in other words, virtually everywhere! Just have one ready, and you won't have to worry.

> **"** *The road to Hades is easy to travel.* **"**
>
> —BION

✓ Collapsible Shovel

A good quality collapsible shovel is useful, if not essential, for digging out of mud, ditches, and loose sand. They're also ideal for burying things—horrible, smelly, unmentionable things.

✓ Bag of Sand

For emergency traction, as in mud, snow, or ice, throw some sand in front of the wheels. It will give you the grip you need to get going.

✓ Extra Set of Car Keys

Put them in one of those magnetic cases under the bumper. And then don't tell the guy you just met in the bar. But *do* tell everyone else in the car.

✓ Steering Wheel Lock

And other security devices (remember: extra keys!): believe it or not, some people may actually want to steal your steed. So lock up, remove your valuables from the car, and check out www.securityworld.com for options.

✓ Electronic Toll Pass

ETP is a great way to speed the journey through toll plazas and reduce the need to scramble under seat cushions for lost quarters and crumpled dollar bills that could be better spent on cold beverages from vending machines. Check out websites if you're traveling across state lines or are unfamiliar with how the toll system works. Trust me, it's worth the extra effort when you speed to the head of the line through rush hour traffic. You'll slow, pass, and go as other, less prepared drivers wait in long lines to pay their toll.

√ Radar Detectors

OK, you need to drive safely within speed limits at all times. Got that? Doing so keeps you law abiding and prevents unwanted delays as you Trip along the highway. It's also more fuel efficient, safer, and, hey, it's the law. There. We said it. The rest is up to you. Besides, these puppies are illegal in many states, so be sure to check local ordinances or risk confiscation.

√ First-Aid Kit

Heaven forbid, but have it anyway. You can buy a compact first-aid kit for your car at most any large drug store or auto store. And don't think strictly Red-Cross first aid; I'd throw buttons, a sewing kit, sunscreen, and condoms into the pack . . . just because.

Roll Your Own

If you want to make a first-aid kit of your own, these items should get you through any rough spots, including some non-vehicular disasters:

Your Bare-Bones First-Aid Kit

Eye drops
Antacids
Laxatives
Cotton-tipped swabs
Sterile bandages
Band-Aids
Legal pain relief of your choice: aspirin, ibuprofen, naproxen
Topical antibiotic cream or treated wipes
Tissues
Sterile latex gloves
Tweezers
Hand sanitizer
Nail scissors
Matches or lighter (for sterilization)
Nasal spray
Blanket
Penlight (with new batteries)
Gauze
Elastic bandage
Surgical tape

✓ Sunglasses

What can I say? Sunglasses are *the* essential accessory to the total Road Trip "look," both in and out of the car. Squinting can be taxing whether it's from the morning sun or last evening's tequila shooters. And who can deny their cool quotient? In fact, shades really should come right after gasoline and music on the Road Tripper's list of "most important stuff."

Oh, and by the way, when you're driving you really need glare and UV protection, too. So make sure you have shades with polarized lenses—in stylish, outlaw frames, naturally! Brown, amber, and grey are the most protective lens colors. Are you not sure if your cheap sunglasses qualify as roadworthy sun blockers? Visit www.sunglassassociation.com for the 411.

DETOUR

These boots were made for . . .
. . . comfortable driving. Anything with a heel makes it easier on your pedal foot when it's your turn to drive. The best? Cowboy boots.

✓ Bathing Suit

That your Road Trip takes place in January has nothing to do with needing a bathing suit. Not only are there year-round hot tubs and spas from sea to shining sea, but sometimes a really, really successful Road Trip can take an unscheduled tropical detour; if you play your cards right, that is. Plus, a bathing suit takes up virtually no room, so leaving it behind is plain unnecessary. Don't forget the sun block either: SPF 30 or better, especially if you're Tripping in a convertible in the summer. I mean, really!

√ Hat

Of course, you may not start out Tripping in a fancy convertible, or plan on driving anywhere near a beach, but those aren't the only reasons to have a good, tight-fitting hat with some sort of brim. You never know when Lady Luck is just around the corner and you might not finish your Road Trip in the car you started in or end up in the place you thought you would, no matter what your mother said. Hats are also useful disguises; enough said!

√ Cooler

Ah, nitty-gritty time. Whether it is large, small, lunch-sized, rolling, plastic, Styrofoam, or soft, no Road Trip should begin without a well-stocked cooler. And it's not at all unusual or unwarranted to have several in one car. A new option takes advantage of the latest technology; it's an insulated, plug-in iceless cooler powered by your car's cigarette lighter (or, in newer cars, one of the myriad auxiliary electrical outlets placed throughout the vehicle.) Some of the fancier new coolers can also function in reverse and keep things warm, which is nice for snacks. You can find one for about $100. Once you buy one, all you'll have to decide is which is more important—cold beer or hot nachos. Road Tripping just got better.

But here's the bottom line on coolers. They are a primary packing concern, and their integral placement in the vehicle takes precedence over most everything else, like underwear and warm clothing. Just make sure—whether it's right up front, in the trunk, or in the "way back"—you can get at your cooler easily. You don't want to dig through unimportant detritus such as underpants when you're desperate to replenish.

√ Maps

Have I mentioned how important maps are? I don't care if the Road Trip you're planning has no destination, somewhere along the way, you're going to need a map; a really good, detailed road map. And make sure it's up to date. Nothing's more frustrating than finding out that the road you intended to travel is closed, or that the scenic village you intended to spend the night in is not on the map. So before you head off into Tripper heaven, buy yourself a brand-new road atlas. But first check it out carefully: I once got completely lost because the Internet map atlas I had wasn't accurate at all.

And speaking of maps, don't forget that every Trip begins with a Tunes Captain (next entry) and a "Mapper." The Mapper is your navigator: he or she holds the map, the course, and your happiness. Please make sure this person knows how to read a map and can direct with conviction. So many fellow Trippers seem to know better, even without a map. Sheesh. In the Tripocracy, only the Mapper can tell the driver where to turn or which road to take. It's the law.

√ Music

Music is an absolute, critical must: always take it seriously, and always be prepared. Music can be provided by your own personal collection of CDs, tapes, or, best and most preferred, that musical miracle, the iPod and its various relations. Did I mention the Tunes Captain's nemesis, the old-fashioned (pre-satellite) car radio? You must at least have a good working car radio and working auto antenna. Don't ever rely on a hootenanny in your quest for old-fashioned fun. It's got to be prerecorded music, jocko, because of course you'll sing along; you still want to sound your best. When it comes to music on a Road Trip there's only one true and stead-fast rule: don't leave home without it.

MP3 players with power conver-sion kits are the most efficient way to carry thousands of songs on a long jaunt. It's so easy to create custom play lists that the CD is just about dead. Now your entire Road Trip can have its own sound track! Think of memories that a certain special mix will evoke, long after the Road Trip ends. You'll always be able to relive your journey.

Some Trippers may want to add satellite radio to their musical montage. Sirius, XM, and WorldSpace are the three satellite radio broadcasters currently offering hundreds of stations with dozens of genres, from music to news to sports and beyond. Satellite radio's #1 feature, though, is its spectacular digital quality, relayed by satellite, which allows the listener to remain perfectly tuned to the same station from Boston to San Diego, Seattle to Key West.

Remember, too, that people are extremely protective of their own music libraries and personal preferences. Back in the day, you went through the roof if someone changed "your" radio station, but we've got CD collections and iPods to contend with now. So employ the "ask before you touch" rule when it comes to music on the road, whether changing the stations or going through other people's stuff. Before you even start your engine, appoint a Tunes Captain (it's usually the driver). The Tripocracy demands that the Tunes Captain rules when it comes to sound.

CALIFORNIA
boasts both the highest and lowest points in the continental U.S.—100 miles from each other. Mount Whitney tops off at 14,495 feet and Bad Water in Death Valley is 282 feet below sea level.

✓ TP (Toilet Paper to You)
That's right. You'll thank me when you've got something better than a bunch of Arby's napkins for the purpose. Look in your drugstore's "travel-size" section, too. Today you'll find they sell little TP-for-one packets. How handy is that?

✓ Pencil and Paper
It'll come in handy, trust me. Especially as you drive away from the gas station where you just got a set a complicated directions and your Mapper says, "OK. Anybody get that?"

✓ THE LITTLE ROAD TRIP HANDBOOK
'Nuff said.

CHAPTER 3

10 THINGS YOU MUST NEVER BRING ON A ROAD TRIP

Or, Your Mother, Bad Perfume, and
8 Other Essential No-Nos

When setting out on an adventure designed to celebrate the unfettered freedom of the road and the endlessly entertaining lightness
of being, what you don't carry is at least as important as what you
do. You sure as hell don't want to load up with a lot of complicated
baggage—not the nylon duffle variety and not the emotional kind,
either. I can't emphasize the "emotional baggage" part enough. You
need to exorcise your own demon Louis Vuittons and be sure not
to bring any aboard via your fellow Trippers. It would be counter–
Road Trip to have to leave your onetime best friend on the highway
drifting like flotsam and jetsam on a sea of ill will.

According to the bylaws of Tripocracy, you're on the road to
leave your cares behind. Therefore, you must never bring any of
the following items along with you on a Road Trip; they are all
items best left behind.

1. Your Mother

Or anyone else's either for that matter. Yes, I know, even Pamela
Anderson is somebody's mother, but really, be sensible. On the

other hand, the good news is that Pamela Anderson is not *your* mother, or your Road Mates' either, so she is indeed eligible to join you on your jaunt.

2. Unapproved Fragrances

The dizzying, piney scent of the great outdoors . . . a cheeseburger, grilled to perfection . . . the briny verve of the salt sea spray. To some, Chanel No. 5 stirs the senses; to others, a fine Cuban cigar evokes romance. So you might want to make a short list of what's what in the Road Trip Smell Department: deodorant, yes; patchouli, no; a nice mint julep? Yummy. You get the picture. If you think you can just seat the nasally offensive Trippers next to each other, think again. Make your list of what smells you can stand and what's verboten. Unless you want to deal with the consequences, that sort of idiosyncrasy has got to be respected. Decisions are unanimous in the Tripocracy. Remember: sweet smells are fleeting, but stink sticks.

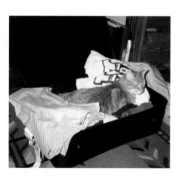

3. Animals (This Includes Your Cat)

No animals are ever allowed on any Road Trip. Not a docile little parakeet who never squawks peep one. Not a tiny sleeping puppy in a little doggy bed. No gentle giant anaconda as sweet as your old granny. I don't care where they

usually sit when you're driving, because they aren't getting in the car. No pet will be able to withstand the frenzy and hoopla that grows exponentially once you really get your Trippin' on. Full-blown Road Trip frenzy will ruffle any animal's feathers, not to mention yours, so it's not fair to them or to you: leave your pets at home. Oh, if you're still having second thoughts, refer back to Item #2: consider the smell factor.

4. Illegal Anything

Possession, use, or cavalier flaunting of illegal stuff, which has not been unanimously preapproved is grounds for mid-Trip roadside abandonment. You can and will be dropped off in the middle of nowhere if caught. Many Road Trippers establish rules on this point beforehand, and it's generally agreed that no dissenting vote is allowed. What if you had planned a rowdy rout, only to be surprised by a Trip Mate who turns out to be some sort of neo-ethicist ringer? Now there's a mistake you won't get a chance to make twice. You want to get home eventually with everybody still talking to each other and nobody in jail? No illegal anything.

5. Blackberry

Now here's a rule with a built-in exception. Things do happen. Occasionally information does need to be traded: that's just Murphy's law. Consequently, one all-team master PDA that lists PINs, credit card numbers, integral route info (like folks with free food, drink, and lodging along the way), and emergency data can be kept and guarded in a single receptacle, like the ever-useful glove compartment. It should only be visible in emergencies, and business related e-mails should never be considered emergencies on any Road Trip.

Free Food on the Road

Grab any free edibles you can pick up on the road and, no, I don't mean dead possums, armadillos, or other road kill. Laugh if you like, but after a bad night in Atlantic City, free food samples, such as crackers, jams and jellies, mints, and the like, could become your next three-course dinner.

6. Contagious Diseases

Uh, no: *nyet, nein, nunca, jamais, non.* Need I say more? OK, wait. There are two possible exceptions to the rule: if the team agrees, the common cold may tag along. And, though not necessarily contagious, a severe case of gastrointestinal distress—especially one with noxious overtones—should be discouraged. Insidious, GI distress often casts an unavoidable and inconvenient pall on the Road Trip experience.

7. Camera

COLORADO *is the Land of the Thirsty: it has more microbreweries per capita than any other state.*

Ah, now it really gets tough to leave things behind, no? But if you're of real Road Tripper caliber, you know that your memories, however dim, will suffice. Photographs and video footage are just litigation waiting to happen. So put away that camera phone. Now!

8. Trouble (a.k.a. Baggage)

Here are just a few of the many things no one wants to hear about:

- A relative or old friend you feel responsible for
- Work-related bullshit politics
- Funky physical problems
- Funky psychological problems
- Serious, paralyzing heartache—heartache so bad it defies all fun, heartache so bad it can bend spoons
- Legal entanglements
- Your recent bankruptcy filing
- Your ex

9. Jail Bait

Well, yes, technically it means an underage female; but anyone that might a) raise suspicion on the road among the authorities or b) compromise the F.Q. (Fun Quotient) and integrity of the Trip are not welcome and should be avoided.

This means not only young girls, even if they have grown up in a most delightful way, but also a spouse who doesn't belong to you, a felon, a mooch, a tattletale, and a thief. Mark my words; you're better off without them. Still confused? Re-read "Trouble," #8, above, and commit to memory.

10. Weapons

I mean, this is a Road Trip. One more beer should be your weapon of choice (unless you're driving, of course!). No firearms, swords, stun guns, mortars, or grenades. No lasers or Tasers. Legal, multi-purpose cutlery serves a purpose in case of emergency, so the guy with the Swiss Army knife can come. The AK-47 stays behind; really, regardless of whether you're headed to a renaissance fair or a civil war encampment.

" The safest road to hell is the gradual one—the gentle slope, soft underfoot, without sudden turnings, without milestones, without signposts. "

—CLIVE STAPLES LEWIS

CHAPTER 4

SAVING THE BENJAMINS

And the Lincolns and Washingtons, Too

There's no need to spend your last dime to have a ton of fun. American ingenuity, combined with somebody in the car always being sober enough to drive and put the kibosh on the purchase of too many high-price pita chips, will help keep the Road Trip coffers full enough for plenty of hijinx. Nevertheless, there's always room for a few tips on saving some dough in the right places, so you can spend it all on commemorative shot glasses, cheap wine, and the occasional call home to stave off the fears of your loved ones. Here they are:

Pump Your Own Gas

It'll still save you a few cents per gallon, but the truth is it's getting harder and harder to run across the friendly, old-fashioned gas station where you even have the option of service. Gone are the days when you'd hear the "Ding-Ding!" as your car rode over that rubber hose as you drove up to the pump. So, you'll need to know what kind of fuel to use (that means gasoline vs. diesel as well as the octane rating). Check that owner's manual if you're not sure, because you don't want to buy premium when regular will do just fine. It's like pouring beer on the floor, that's what a waste of money it is.

Snacks

It's not just for beer and soda anymore. The cooler you've got tucked into your trunk should be big enough to hold salsa, cold cuts, mayo, peanut butter & jelly, cheese—or all the ingredients for any of your favorite snacks that you might otherwise be tempted to pick up along the way. When you do stop to replenish your supplies, shop at regular grocery stores instead of more expensive delis or minimarts at gas stations. And, whenever physically, emotionally, and mentally possible, prepare your own snack concoctions and/or sandwiches instead of buying them ready-made. Now you're saving money.

Cash Stash

It's easy to get carried away when you *are* away. Why, one stop at South of the Border, and you could blow it all. Best plan I've found is to decide on a daily wad to spend before you take off, and stick to the cash in your pocket.

The Daily Banker

If you really don't trust yourself, make someone the daily Banker, and have him hold your credit cards. It's not that he's supposed to be the spending police, but you do think twice if the card's not in your own pocket. It's easy to return home with a bunch of stuff you don't really want. (And just how are you going to explain the Hooters T-shirt?) Believe me, it works. And it's all part of the Tripocracy, so relax.

Don't Bring a Date

A date can cost you. And it can *cost* you. I'm just sayin'.

DETOUR

Free Air Conditioning!

Any nonwinter Road Trip is going to be full of hot spots, so a good trick is to bring *muchos bandannas*. Wet a bandanna, partially wring it out, and tie it loosely around your neck—it'll cool you off in a nanosecond. Even better: if you've got a cooler going, ice up a few bandannas in the cooler. *Brrr*—wintry! *Caution:* if you're wearing a light color, make sure it's an old bandanna, or the colors may run onto your clothes; I know, I've been there.

B.Y.O.B.

Not that we're promoting drinking and driving here, but it's always good to have your own hooch for after-driving enjoyment and relaxation. Since you often don't know where you'll end up at the end of the day, at least you know you'll have your old friend Jack and a couple of cold ones waiting upon your arrival. Of course, it's illegal to carry any open liquor in the car, so be prepared to finish what you start before you get back on the road. And keep all unopened booze stored safely in the trunk of your car.

Don't Pimp Your Ride

Or rather, take the ride that fits the Trip. Now that doesn't mean you have to ride Flintstone-style, with no AC or a crummy sound system—that would be un-American—but there's no need to take an SUV when there's just two of you, either. Gas prices are high, and parking garages are outrageously expensive. This is not about cruising down the main drag and picking up a date for Saturday night; the best car for the job is one that's comfortable, affordable,

and will get you there and back again with relative ease and absolute safety. And remember, a convertible *always* saves on gas, since the air conditioning is free.

Doggie Bags

While on a Road Trip, whenever you eat in restaurants or bars, make sure you make the most of it. Free crackers, pickles, mints—well, sure, naturally. Those little containers of jam you were going throw away from this morning's muffin?

They're perfect on those aforementioned crackers. You should know this stuff by now. But you may not know one of the premiere road rules: "No Food Left Behind." Chinese food, pizza, leftover Buffalo wings, any tidbit you might have left on your plate, are all foods that I promise will be extremely valuable later and another reason to think about investing in the best cooler you can afford. Don't be proud: just say yes to the doggie bag.

CONNECTICUT *enacted the first speed limit law in 1901, at twelve miles per hour. On a brighter legal note, it was one of only two states that refused to ratify the Prohibition law.*

Mileage & Reward Points

Here's where your credit cards really come into play. Think of all the business trips, expensive dinners, and birthday gifts you have to buy all year long. Don't you deserve payback? That's why they invented reward points. These babies are gold on a Road Trip. You can get free nights at hotel chains, for starters. And best of all, you can even *rent a car* to drive on your Road Trip, whether or not you have one. Remember that convertible and how it saves on air-conditioning costs? The sheer beauty of it is a joy to behold!

CHAPTER 5

THE ULTIMATE ROAD TRIP MUSIC, MOVIES, AND BOOKS

From Tunes, Titles, and Tomes That Match Your
Mood and Geography to the 10 Best Road Trip Songs
of All Time

The sound track to your Road Trip is so important it gets its own chapter and is as simple as this: without Road Music there is no Road Trip. It is an absolutely essential part of the Road Trip experience. The music makes the miles fly; the friendship fun, and the mood mellow. Whether singing a familiar song you all recall from back in the day or learning to appreciate a whole new musical genre, Road Music is one of the chief pleasures of the Trip.

The 10 Best Road Trip Songs Ever

1. WOODSTOCK (Joni Mitchell)—Yeah, OK, so the tempo is kind of slow; deal with it. What are you even doing in my car if you have to be told this festival of peace, music, and love was *the* Ultimate Road Trip?

2. LOVE SHACK (The B-52's)—
Sex, a great pit stop, a juke box,
and a Road Trip, all rolled into
one fabulous song. And, did I
mention SEX?

3. I WILL SURVIVE (Gloria
Gaynor)—Freedom! Confi-
dence! Heady individualism!
This great song touts everything
the Road Trip stands for!

> **UTAH's**
> *town Levan, which is
> located in the middle of the
> state, is rumored to have
> been named as a joke; it's
> n-a-v-e-l spelled
> backwards.*

4. ALL I WANNA DO (Sheryl Crowe)—and the next four
words of the song are "is have some fun." This song makes
me want to take off and DRIVE (and I got a feeling I'm not
the only one).

5. THE THEME FROM ROUTE 66 (Nelson Riddle & His
Orchestra)—Just listen to the cruisin' strings in the back-
ground and your hands will be twitching for a steering wheel.

6. LOVE THE ONE YOU'RE WITH (Stephen Stills)—But
that's just between us.

7. BORN TO RUN (Bruce Springsteen)—For a billion
excellent reasons, not the least of which is that it stands for
coast-to-coast Rock-&-Roll Road Tripping need.

8. (I Can't Get No) SATISFACTION (The Rolling Stones)—
A true R&R classic, fraught with the sort of angst that makes
one desperate to leave home.

9. ON THE ROAD AGAIN (Willie Nelson)—OK, get this:
here's a guy in pigtails, older than dirt, who looks like he

hasn't taken a bath in thirty years: he goes from C&W newcomer with a pompadour, gets mega rich, goes totally bankrupt, is crushed by the IRS—whereupon all his friends get together to get him out of hock. This is his theme song. And you're worried about taking a couple of days off?

10. 99 BOTTLES OF BEER ON THE WALL (Anonymous)—You know it's going to happen. Just give in to it.

Must-Have Songs for Your Road Trip Mix

Guerrilla Road Trippers aren't partial to any one type of music. They just "get it": a song is either Road Trip worthy or not; genre doesn't matter. Some picks for all-time cuts include the following:

BORN TO BE WILD (Steppenwolf)—The theme of this book!

ROUTE 66 (Chuck Berry or The Rolling Stones)—You can't make a wrong turn with this Road Trip classic.

FUN, FUN, FUN (The Beach Boys)—Because it is.

THUNDER ROAD (Bruce Springsteen)—An invitation you can't refuse.

SIX DAYS ON THE ROAD (Dave Dudley)—Another great trucker tune from an all-time C&W star.

HAWAII 5-0 THEME (The Ventures)—Maui wowee.

I GET AROUND (The Beach Boys again)—Iconic.

CALIFORNIA GIRLS (The Beach Boys)—A love song to the entire USA.

I DROVE ALL NIGHT (Roy Orbison)—Totally cool song with Roy's eerie voice.

ONLY IN AMERICA (Jay and the Americans)—Forget Toby Keith, this song mixes innocence, optimism, and American pride. All of which holds up just fine, thank you very much!

RAMBLIN' MAN/MIDNIGHT RIDER (The Allman Brothers Band)—Have you ever been to a good bar where one of these *wasn't* on the jukebox?

I'VE BEEN EVERYWHERE (Johnny Cash)—Even more poignant and powerful now that the "Man in Black" is dead.

KING OF THE ROAD (Roger Miller)—He makes it all seem so effortless. Miller's a great, underrated artist.

ROAD (Nick Drake)—Put the top down or roll back the moon roof, and take a slow ride under the stars with someone you love—or want to love—with this dreamy song playing. Bingo!

FREE RIDE (The Edgar Winter Group)—Loud, raucous, and trashy . . . just like a well-executed Road Trip.

FREEBIRD (Lynyrd Skynyrd)—Now, we're talkin' *free*.

LITTLE RED CORVETTE (Prince)—It's a car, after all.

BROWN SUGAR (The Rolling Stones)—You should play it just around midnight.

LOUIE, LOUIE (The Kingsmen)— Play this one extra loud one time for me, won't you please? Don't you just love that cheesy Farfisa organ sound?

LOLA (The Kinks)—A one-size-fits-all gender bender classic.

SECRET AGENT MAN (Johnny Rivers)—Power, danger, and sexuality all shaken, never stirred.

TRUCKIN' (The Grateful Dead)—Does this really require any explanation?

WISCONSIN

was the birthplace in 1959 of Barbara Millicent Roberts, known to her enormous circle of friends as Barbie. She was born in fictional Willows, where she attended Willows High School before moving to New York City.

AQUARIUS/LET THE SUNSHINE IN (The 5th Dimension)—A 1960s classic that seems so earnest and innocent by today's standards that it just may make you want to cry. Don't.

GOT TO GIVE IT UP (Marvin Gaye)—For when it's time to get it on.

HOLIDAY (Madonna)—From one of the all-time great pop tarts.

ALL ALONG THE WATCHTOWER (Jimi Hendrix)—Crank up the wailing guitar solo.

BEAUTIFUL DAY (U2)—If only for the power and glory of Edge's guitar.

SATURDAY NIGHT'S ALRIGHT FOR FIGHTING (Elton John)—Pedal to the metal, people. Just watch the radar detector when this one comes on!

DAYTRIPPER (The Beatles)—This song's conducive to off-key sing-a-longs, which is another big reason why you should audition your Trip Mates before setting off.

CROSSROADS/I FEEL FREE (Cream)—Read the titles again.

GOOD RIDDANCE (TIME OF YOUR LIFE) (Green Day)—What the Road Trip should be.

TAKE IT EASY (Jackson Brown or The Eagles)—Oh, we got it eeeeeeecca—sy?

25 Really Good Geographically Specific Tunes

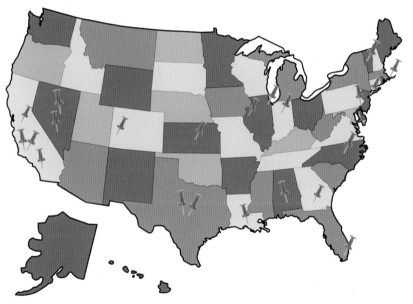

CALIFORNIA DREAMIN'—The Mamas & the Papas
YELLOW ROSE OF TEXAS—Mitch Miller and the Gang
MOONLIGHT IN VERMONT—Ella Fitzgerald and Louis Armstrong

ROCKY MOUNTAIN HIGH—John Denver
TAKE ME HOME, COUNTRY ROADS—John Denver
I LEFT MY HEART IN SAN FRANCISCO—Tony Bennett
SAN FRANCISCO (YOU'VE GOT ME)—The Village People
WICHITA LINEMAN—Glen Campbell
DO YOU KNOW WHAT IT MEANS
TO MISS NEW ORLEANS?—
Louis Armstrong
GARY, INDIANA (REPRISE)—
Ron Howard
THE GRAND CANYON
SUITE—New York Philharmonic
OLD CAPE COD—Patti Page
THEME FROM *NEW YORK, NEW
YORK*—Frank Sinatra or Liza Minnelli
KANSAS CITY—B.B. King
SWEET HOME ALABAMA—Lynyrd Skynyrd
VIVA LAS VEGAS—Elvis or ZZ Top
MOON OVER MIAMI—Eddie Duchin and his Orchestra
I'VE GOT A GAL IN KALAMAZOO—Glenn Miller
Orchestra
CHICAGO—Frank Sinatra
GEORGIA ON MY MIND—Ray Charles
PHILADELPHIA FREEDOM—Elton John
ALABAMA—Neil Young
CAROLINA IN MY MIND—James Taylor
DO YOU KNOW THE WAY TO SAN JOSE?—Dionne
Warwick
IS ANYBODY GOING TO SAN ANTONE—Doug Sahm

OREGON

has the only state flag that's different on both sides. The state seal is on one side and a beaver, the state animal, is on the reverse.

Musical Categories

Just a reminder checklist so you don't forget to bring your favorites from home.

Rock & Roll	Ska	Lounge
Pop	Heavy Metal	Big Band
Country	Classical	Soul
Alt-Country	Jazz	Funk
Blue Grass	Opera	Gospel
Americana	Girl Bands	R&B
EMO	Boy Bands	Show Tunes
Hip-Hop	Polka	Reggatone
Folk	Reggae	Klezmer

Homework We Love: The Road Flick

I'm not referring to the old "Road Movies" starring Bob Hope and Bing Crosby from way back when, although they are a hoot and precursors to many of today's favorites. I am talking about a bunch of great films that see the Road as god, just as we do. You may take watching these flicks below as serious homework or, in those times when you're hearing the siren song of the road in your head but you just can't get away, enjoy any of these for sweet relief.

Easy Rider—This may be the first movie that comes to mind when thinking about the Road Trip movie genre. About freedom, counterculture, drugs, motorcycles, and Mardi Gras, it's no wonder this is a timeless favorite. Watch again if you haven't seen it in a while; Nicholson is as cool today as he ever was.

Almost Famous—Let's see, a movie that about a rock 'n' roll band on the road. Could it get any better than this? I think not.

Thelma & Louise—This original girl buddy movie (with Brad Pitt, too!) never gets old, and the last scene never seems to lose its heroism. Period.

Two for the Road—Starring a young and sexy Albert Finney coupled with the chic ingénue goddess Audrey Hepburn as they travel in and out of love all over 1960s Europe. This oldie but goodie is one of the great underrated heartstring-pullers and scenery chewing blockbusters.

Bonnie & Clyde—Not generally considered a Road Flick, but boy oh boy, and it all takes place in a car.

The Wizard of Oz—Dorothy was too young to drive, and her pals weren't really eligible for a license. Yet this is a real contender for the best Road Flick of all time. After all, it's the ultimate Trip.

North by Northwest—OK, not technically a Road Flick either, but jeez, Cary Grant did get a around. He got laid on a train, climbed Mount Rushmore, and hung out at that fabulous house with its incredible view.

O Brother, Where Art Thou?—A send-up of the original Road Trip literary blockbuster Homer's *Odyssey*—written some time before the advent of cinema—this is great fun and a real Road Trip, too.

Rain Man—This film represents the nightmare of what it might be like if your mother made you bring your little brother along on your Road Trip—only take this times a million.

Pee-Wee's Big Adventure—On our best days we couldn't hope to be on this nutty of a Trip. You can watch and be either glad or sad.

Around the World in 80 Days—The most extensive Road Trip possible, of course. See the 1956 version, which is, incidentally, the first movie I ever saw.

Any James Bond Movie—maybe it's just me, but really, the Aston Martin? The inside scoop on what's hot in every port—and a babe in each one of them—I bow to the master.

Bagdad Café—A roadside stop, lederhosen, Jack Palance, a magic act, and one of the best title songs ever composed for the movies.

There are many, many excellent runner-ups, of course, and if you're on a roll, you may want to consider the movie actually named *Road Trip*. And plenty of others, like *Breakdown, The Straight Story, My Own Private Idaho, National Lampoon's Vacation, It Happened One Night*; the list goes on and on. I guess there are as many as the amount of time you have to waste until you can get back on the Road yourself.

Armchair Road Tripping
Books That Bring the Road Trip Home

Whether you're at home or in the office and dreaming of that great escape, it's often easier to hide out with a book than to slip something into the DVD player and risk discovery. Here are a few classics and favorites.

On the Road, by Jack Kerouac
The bible of the Beat Generation, and the title says it all, doesn't it? Kerouac is the master, and there are those who will insist that this is the original Road Trip.

Horatio's Drive: America's First Road Trip, by Dayton Duncan and Ken Burns
This is the book about the $50 bet mentioned in the introduction.

Travels with Charley: In Search of America, by John Steinbeck
A man. A dog. A Road Trip. Author John Steinbeck set out in 1960 on a three-month tour across America with his poodle, Charley, to answer the question we all still ask every time we hit the highway: "What are Americans like today?" (Oh, the dog is allowed in this case, because it is the *only* passenger. Who's to complain?)

Electric Kool-Aid Acid Test, by Tom Wolfe
It's the sixties, man, and Ken Kesey and the Merry Pranksters are living life through the wonders of chemistry—namely, running around the country in a Day-Glo bus doing LSD. That's like being on the Road in a time warp.

Fear and Loathing in Las Vegas: A Savage Journey to the Heart of the American Dream, by Hunter S. Thompson

More drugs; more Road Tripping; but this time we're in the playground of the Western world: Las Vegas, and Thompson's gonzo journalism is just heating up.

Roadfood, by Jane and Michael Stern

The indefatigable Sterns have revised their classic volume on all the yummiest spots to chow down from coast-to-coast. Pay attention, they know what they're talking about.

Road Trip USA: Cross-Country Adventures of America's Two-Lane Highways, by Jamie Jensen

A totally fun travel guide that makes use of the forgotten roads that are home to some top-notch Americana.

Road Trip America: A State-by-State Tour Guide to Offbeat Destinations, by Andrew F. Wood

When you're looking for the weirdest, looniest, most fun roadside attractions from sea to shining sea, this is the book to take along.

Weird U.S.: Your Travel Guide to America's Local Legends and Best Kept Secrets, by Mark Moran and Mark Sceurman

The guys who started with *Weird N.J.* have gone national, with more nutty legends, people, and forgotten spots not to miss once you get behind the wheel.

Route 66: The Mother Road, by Michael Wallis

A colorful, nostalgic look at America's favorite and most-loved road—the only highway so great it's an entire Road Trip in and of itself.

CHAPTER 6
WHAT IS (AND ISN'T) A ROAD TRIP

Get That Car Seat Outta the Back, Brother: A Very Particular Set of Standards to Keep Your Trip Pure

A Road Trip isn't a Road Trip just because you hopped in the car, because it's Saturday, and most definitely *not* just because you call it one. Like traveling around in the real world, Road Trip requirements are stringent and strict, and abusers should be punished without delay. Of course Road Trippers understand that the punishment should fit the crime.

" *Though we travel the world over to find the beautiful, we must carry it with us or we find it not.* **"**
—RALPH WALDO EMERSON

DETOUR

Everybody's got their own baggage.

No, really. Everyone brings their own stuff. But get a few containers—plastic milk cartons, clear boxes with snap-on tops—to store communal things, like food and drink, music, first-aid kit, blankets and pillows, etc. That way nobody has to bother a buddy for access to a private stash.

- Any car with a child in it is not on a Road Trip. Period. End of story. Listen: feel free to travel with children, but don't confuse any such journey with a true Road Trip.

- It does give the Trip a little *frisson* of excitement if someone is trying to escape from something. Running away is so damn exciting!

- The Road Trip is, by its very nature, pointless. One usually ends up back where one started out, but not always. Occasionally there is an end game to the Trip—a party, a natural phenomenon, a freebie, or a celebrity—but the Road Trip discourages things meaningfully productive. It is the gestalt of the Trip that makes it so . . . thrilling, so carefree, and so naughty. Hence our motto: *it's the journey, not the destination.*

- Road Trips are spontaneous. Planning a few stops upon the way does not negate the spontaneity of the Trip. It's all about the kind of stops. You'll know in your heart when you've sinned.

- Road Trips are pet-free zones. I love a little kitty cat. We all do. It belongs at home watching the news with your old aunt, not on the road.

- Road Trips are loud. There are things you say on a Road Trip—stuff that flies out of your mouth before you know it: "No, turn here!" "Turn that song up!" "We've got to stop there!" It's all about transportation with an exclamation point. On a Road Trip, silence is not golden. It is anathema. It is failure.

So once again, with feeling:

"It's the journey, not the destination."

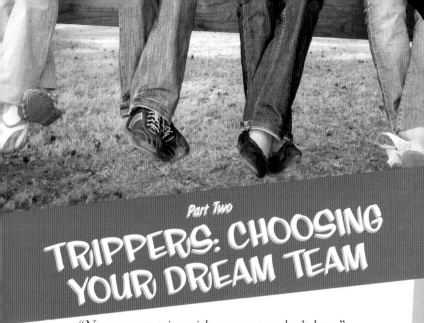

Part Two

TRIPPERS: CHOOSING YOUR DREAM TEAM

"Never go on trips with anyone you don't love."
—ERNEST HEMINGWAY

Travel is a true test of friendship, and it's often been said that if you are still friends with someone after you've take a long trip together chances are good that you'll be friends for life. It's almost impossible to hide your true self on a Road Trip, which is one of the joys (or horrors) of Tripping. Choose your fellow Trippers well; you don't want any of them to become a roadside hazard.

Your Trip Mates are the people with whom you will share not only your road cruising dream but also some very close quarters. The best music, the sweetest ride, and the most idyllic scenery can all be for naught if you don't have the right posse. So exercise caution, my friends. Do go with your instincts: if a little alarm in your head starts to ring when your friend asks to take along her outpatient cousin from Kalamazoo, by all means, put on the brakes.

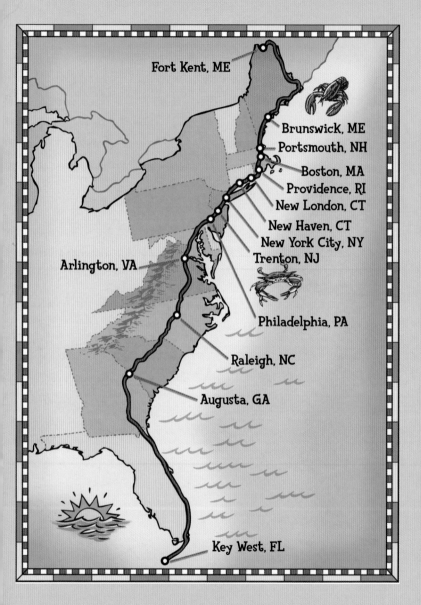

Fort Kent, ME

Brunswick, ME
Portsmouth, NH
Boston, MA
Providence, RI
New London, CT
New Haven, CT
New York City, NY
Trenton, NJ

Arlington, VA

Philadelphia, PA

Raleigh, NC

Augusta, GA

Key West, FL

CLASSIC ROAD TRIP #2—US 1: EAST COAST

Highway 1, or US 1, will take care of all your East Coast desires. It runs all the way from Fort Kent, Maine, on the Canadian border, to the buoy at the southernmost point in Key West, Florida, and is exactly 2,390 miles long. The fact that the newer Interstate 95 either follows the same route or closely parallels US 1 proves that highway builders got it right the first time. In fact, the folks living down in the Florida Keys rightly call it "The Road to Paradise." Key West is actually marked "Mile 0."

What's along the way? The beauty of US I—besides the fact that it isn't I-95—is that it connects a bunch of great cities with some of the most spectacular scenery in the East. Where else in the world can you party in South Beach; motor past Tara-like plantations in Georgia; protest in Washington, D.C.; see a Broadway play in New York, New York; travel the Boston Post Road in Connecticut (the same road the colonists used to deliver mail between Boston and New York back in the day); hit Boston for a Red Sox game; stop in Portland, Maine, for some Down East lobsters; and even cross into another country at its terminus (would that be marked "Mile 2,390?"). There's plenty to tickle any Road Tripper's fancy. And if you're just armchair traveling, check out Berenice Abbott's pictures from her very own 1954 Road Trip on US 1.

Chapter 7
THE INTERVIEW
Or, Simple Ways to Spot a Loser

OK, so it's not exactly an interview, but sometimes you will find yourself considering asking someone along that you don't know all that well. You can't expect to have them step into your office (though you might be able to read his résumé on his face), but it's a good idea to take him out for a beer, or show him your car, chat him up, and sneak in some questions about music (perhaps the ultimate testing ground).

Here's a checklist of questions to subtly and deftly work into the conversation. Give one point for each question answered in the affirmative, and keep score for the best results:

- Is he prone to carsickness or any other stomach disorders?
- Does she have to ride with the window open or the top down?
- Does he have to check with his office, wife, mother, or therapist first?
- Does he have any outstanding warrants? Have you seen his picture on the wall of your post office?
- Does she carry any contagious diseases?
- Does he stare at your crotch/breasts throughout the interview? (And do you think this is good or bad?)
- Does he constantly consult his watch; flip open his cell phone; check his Blackberry; wipe, pick, or scratch his nose; tug at a wedgie; blink; or remind you that he needs to be home at a certain time?
- Does she remind you of your mother?
- Does she want to discuss her allergies before the Trip?
- Does he want to bring a pet? If yes, is it a ferret?
- Has her driver's license expired?
- Has he inquired as to whether anybody will be bringing a steam iron?
- Does he say he can't really drive at night?
- Does he admit to bed-wetting?
- Has she asked whether she can have her own room on the road? Has she already planned on bringing her own pillow?
- Does he start sentences with "My Mom and I . . . " or "Kabbalah says . . ."?
- Has she forgotten her wallet?

TEXAS *has a single ranch—the King Ranch—that is larger than the state of Rhode Island.*

- Does he smoke clove cigarettes?
- Has she ever had vertigo?
- Is he afraid of the water?
- Has he discussed at length his special dietary needs?
- Does she faint at the sight of blood?
- And, most importantly, did he not ask one single question about you?

LOSER LOOKOUT

Will this potential Road Tripper totally ruin your Road Trip? How many times did you get "yes" to one of the above questions?

1–9: Inquire if potential Road Tripper might agree to etiquette and hygiene classes upfront. Even dog obedience school would help.

10–14: Better hope he doesn't end up as your roommate.

15–19: Consider last-minute change of plans—perhaps that round-the-world tour of holy grottos with your old aunt.

20–23: You'd have a better time staying home and renting Road Trip movies.

Clearly, if he answers "yes" to any of these queries, he should be immediately disqualified. Don't even think twice about it: "Yes" means no.

> *"There ain't no surer way to find out whether you like people or hate them than to travel with them."*
>
> —MARK TWAIN

The Pros and Cons

You're all set to have the time of your life. Then it suddenly becomes apparent that the proper research hasn't been done, and you find that your car is quite possibly still full of half-wits. People who have *appointments*; someone who's afraid of the *rain*; and another who *hums* incessantly. You find all you want to do is hurry up and get home—and you haven't even left yet!

IDAHO *holds an Annual Spud Day, with the big event being a tug-of-war over a gigantic mashed potato pit.*

You probably shouldn't take either on a Road Trip with you (pros or cons, that is). But, to help you focus your *Road Mate* selection, behold: two checklists—Pro and Con. These should help you get your thoughts together on the kind of person you want riding beside you. Again: *know before you go!* If you find the interview not to your liking, try using this quick and easy pros and cons checklist:

Pros

The following attributes are big pluses for prospects:

Celebrity status
Great car
Knows CPR
Cutting-edge humor
Enormous wealth
Road Trip–experienced
Trust fund baby
Carefree

One-seat-or-less body width

Fabulous wardrobe

Awesome music collection

Toilet-trained

Literate

Drives standard shift car

Friends in high places

Friends in great houses

Not time-sensitive

Legal or medical training

Big spender

Flexible (in attitude, but physical flexibility can also be a plus!)

Great audience

Low morals, high morale

WEST VIRGINIA *is at once thought to be the southernmost northern state, and the northermost southern state.*

" *There is no road or ready way to virtue.* "
—SIR THOMAS BROWNE

Cons

Immediate grounds for disqualification include the following:

Body odor of any type (including bad perfume or cologne)

Poor eyesight

Bad haircut

Contagious

Loves smoking cigars

Owns a Paris Hilton CD

Guilt about persons/work left behind

Firearm aficionado

Narcoleptic
Outstanding warrants
Pussy whipped
Religious zealot
Humorless
Loud talker
Low talker
No talker
Prison tats
Wears a boot knife
Obnoxious laugh
Obsessive-compulsive disorder
Deadbeat
No driver's license
Wears infant in Snuggli-Pak
Flatulence/belching
Loves onions and garlic
   (see body odor above)
Known felon
Road rage/Enrolled in anger
   management classes
Agoraphobic
Stalker
Tone deaf
Bankrupt
Ordained
Unemployed
Mumbles

INDIANA
is home to the first long-distance auto race, now known as Memorial Day weekend's Indianapolis 500. Things have really sped up since the original 75 MPH, $14,000 competition.

CHAPTER 8

TRIPMATES AND THEIR POSITIONS

It's a Tripocracy, and Everyone Has a Job, Whether It's Changing the Music or Reading a Map

Both for comfort and because you really don't want the Trip to dissolve into a sorry mess of micromanagement, there should be only *four* main positions of strength (obviously with fewer than four in the car, everyone except the Driver takes on more responsibility). And every shift should be two hours. That may seem like a short time, but everybody needs to stay in a happy, laid-back mood for a Road Trip to be deemed a success. Change is good. So two hours it is.

Laws of Tripocracy support a well-established hierarchy. We list key positions here. We also list part-time, optional, and emergency positions; but for power and prestige, these are the top jobs.

The Driver

The Wheel Man, the Boss, the Highwayman. Each Driver's prowess and driving style is as unique and different as the number of people behind the wheel. Her finesse with the steering wheel, gas and brake pedal style, and sense of direction are either infused with the touch of an angel or the work of the devil. Either is fine, just know what you want. And remember, the Driver always rules.

There is really only one other steadfast rule about the Driver. But it's huge. Gargantuan. Monumental: *the Driver gets to pick the music and by law also becomes the Tunes Captain.*

Of course, the Navigator is in charge of actually playing the music, but he and the rest of the Trippers are at the mercy of the Driver's musical taste. And, no, exceptions to this rule are not allowed. The work of the Driver is punishing, and her relaxation and happiness is the highest priority. So there will be no poking, no prodding, no fighting, and no biting to express your rage and disappointment. You will grin and bear it, while waiting out the Driver's two-hour stint in stoic silence if you must. You'll be doing your part to assure that the Driver's eyes do not roll into the back of her head by politely listening along to what pleases her. It helps to pretend that you actually like the music she chooses.

Of course, there is a lesson in all this, and it can't be repeated enough: if you don't like the music, use a little more discretion next time in choosing your Trippers.

The Navigator

The Navigator is the most important person in your car, next to the Driver. The Navigator's primary job is to keep the Driver happy, because when your Driver is happy, your whole world becomes a paradise. She'll agree to "go where you want to go, and do what you want to do," as the Mamas and Papas taught us.

The position of "riding shotgun," in the front passenger-side seat, is happily, a term used mostly in a figurative manner these days. Begun as the shotgun-carrying stage coach defenseman, today we might associate the position with road rage. (Remember the ending of *Easy Rider*?) But riding shotgun on a Road Trip as Navigator is strictly all about the karma of the car, and his metaphoric shotgun is pointed at your fellow Trippers to retain your Driver's good nature.

In a full car, with all four of the most important jobs filled by separate Trippers, the Navigator doesn't actually guide the car through the routes, shoals, and channels of the road; the Mapper will do that. Left to navigating in the strictest sense, he will act as DJ, valet, food and beverage manager, ombudsman. But most of all, the Navigator must be completely in sync with the needs of the Driver, a veritable diviner of her needs and desires. Here are just a few things a top-notch Navigator can be expected to be:

Music Man: Music is the lifeblood of a Road Trip. No CD ever plays twice (unless it's *that* good or at the Driver's request); no bad song on the radio sounds more than four notes before it is whisked from the offended ears; and every iPod is tuned to the perfect play list, which is best when preselected and Trip-specific. Most importantly, the Navigator makes sure the Driver hears the music she wants to hear, and *only* the music she wants to hear. It bears repeating: in the world of the Road Trip, the Driver's musical choice is the last word. No commentary from back seat drivers, no questions asked.

Driver Maintenance: Sustenance for the Driver is of the utmost importance. Her mind must be sharp, her thirst slaked, and her belly full. This could require a little forethought. The Navigator needs to be sure the car is stocked with the Driver's favorites before they take their respective positions. Warm drinks, no ice, lack of napkins, a lost bottle opener—so many things might put the Driver off her zone! An edgy, unhappy driver is an unsafe driver. And then whose fault is it when trouble strikes? The Navigator's. Oh yes, this prime car location comes at a price.

Host/Emcee: Though one might think of the Driver as the "host" of the Road Trip, one couldn't be more wrong. The Navigator sets the tone of the Trip and imbues it with *joie de vivre*. In addition, he takes the lead in any matters that would distract the Driver. He must, for example:

• Act as the "Welcome Wagon" for Trippers who may be strangers, or, even dicier intervene when Trippers are a tad too familiar with each other.
• Be a winning conversationalist, regaling all with jokes, ghost

stories, and ribald (but ultimately flattering) tales about the Driver.

- Perform as a caterer/waiter for the entire vehicle. A nice cheese tray, snackie-treats, drinks all around. The Driver is always served first (see above), though she must never be infantilized and should be encouraged to feed herself.
- Referee, and this is a thankless but critical job. A Road Trip is all about fun, so fighting must be nipped in the bud. The "one for all; all for one" watchword that worked so nicely for the Three Musketeers should be the order of the day. Thus, any situation in which a vote might be taken is suggested by and then tallied by the Navigator, unless his name is Chad, in which case this task moves clockwise one position, and somebody else does the counting.

After tending to the immediate needs of the Driver, the next most important aspect of the Navigator's job is keeping the peace. In close quarters, fights happen. Fights over chicks, who saw the cute guy first, who bought the last six-pack, or whose feet smell (or, smell worst). Fights over everything and nothing, really. So you need to reach waaaay back in your mind to your childhood and recall the backhand slap. It was the absolute proof that your mother had eyes in the back of her head, because no matter who was raising hell in the back seat, she could reach her arm back *without even turning* and smack the culprit. Or scold without establishing eye contact. Same skill, different approach.

Look, here's the bottom line: you don't ever want to hear from your Driver what you heard from your parents, *"Don't make me turn this car around!"*

The Mapper

When handled with élan, aplomb, and a kick-ass attitude, this often underappreciated position is at the hub, controlling the thrumming soul of the Trip. Sure, you may occasionally make a wrong turn, and perhaps map-reading isn't your forte, but don't worry, everybody in the car is eventually going to know when you screw up. And they'll screw up later—it's the nature of the beast. But who the hell really cares where you're going? This is why the map has it all over the GPS, that new-fangled stuff lacks humanity. And all that stern direction-giving? No thank you!

NORTH DAKOTA's *town Rugby is the geographical center of North America*

As Mapper you should have all the information necessary to make the Trip go the way *you* want it to go, and all the information should be at your fingertips. When handled skillfully, the Mapper's *can be the true power position*! Here are a few of the responsibilities the Mapper is charged with that put the rest of the Trippers under her thumb—and why the map has it all over a GPS device.

Travel Guide: This puts you in charge of everything from the best burger joint to the hottest clubs. If you're really good and fast on your feet, you can practically design your own city, just by lying! "Gee, no, there are no museums at all in this town," or "Nope, I don't see a coffee bar within thirty miles; but it looks like there's a really great margarita place if you take this next left." These "truths" roll off the tongue of an ace Mapper with remarkable ease. Practice makes perfect!

Emergency Situations: This is where a truly excellent Mapper might well save the day. What if someone is overserved at a bar or party? What if there's a slip-and-fall? Who will find the emergency room? Who will locate the nearest motel for quick recovery? Who knows where the ice machine is? The Mapper. Who will find the bus station when the new friend you've all decided to ask along on the Trip turns out to be a psycho? The Mapper.

> **IOWA**
> *produces more corn than any other state— more than two billion bushels a year*

So, see what I'm saying? The Mapper is tour guide, policeman, emergency medical service provider, and Trip planner. If you think that's not power, think again!

The Point Man

The Point Man is a lookout, the "Land Ho!" watch in the automotive crow's nest, and the creative genius behind the last-minute turn off the road who adds to the overall spontaneity of the Trip. Entire Road Trip legends and successes have hinged on the tightrope-walker agility, ice water veins, and uncanny sixth sense of a Point Man. While the Driver, Navigator, and Mapper have specific tasks, the Point Man's job is to *feel* the road, to find the *soul* of the Trip. He is always making suggestions, pointing out sights, percolating, and predicting, ever ready with the Next Big Idea.

An All-Star Point Man:

- Offers advice on an offbeat location "down the road"
- Takes food and drink orders for in- and out-of-car dining
- Writes down directions

- Relays news and gossip, real, imagined, and unsubstantiated
- Facilitates yesterday's recap, reenacting important events when necessary, embellishing where appropriate, and omitting when prudent
- Acts as spokesperson and arbitrator when situations get dicey, including any encounter with "the authorities"

VERMONT's city of Barre, granite capital of the world, is also home to Hope Cemetery, which features the largest collection of carved Barre gray granite monuments in the world.

" Certainly, travel is more than the seeing of sights; it is a change that goes on, deep and permanent, in the ideas of living. "
—MIRIAM BEARD

Expenses

This is the Point Man's biggest responsibility. There should be a folder or large envelope, along with a pen, to record all the Trip's expenses. Ideally, it's kept in the glove compartment for safe keeping, along with the owner's manual, and insurance card. Many Trippers overlook finances thinking that everything will come out in the wash; the spending will even out. But don't be fooled. It's best to keep track of everyone's contribution so that nobody is cheated and no one feels resentful. Accounting is critical if you've brought a mere acquaintance along or have picked up relative strangers along the way. Keep a log. After all, what could be worse than having a cheapskate or deadbeat with you on a Road Trip? Well, maybe having your therapist.

Event Planning

Overseeing the Fun Quotient is part of the Point Man's job. He should be on the lookout at all times for hilarious stops along the road and on the horizon: the Land of Little Ponies, South of the Border, the Grand Canyon, the Corn Palace, or anything out of the ordinary and potentially diverting and nutty.

"My advice to any traveler who is traveling in order to learn would be: 'Fight tooth and nail to be permitted to travel in what is technically the least efficient way.'"
—ARNOLD TOYNBEE

Part Time, Optional, or Emergency Positions

There are a few alternate positions, some of which are listed just because you might have some extra Trippers on board (the more the merrier). People do love feeling like part of the crew.

Examine your extra Trippers carefully before you embark on your adventure; if their main attraction is that they are mad fun or just plain crazy, then decide right then and there that that will be their only job. They can also be assigned to assist any of the majors (Driver, Navigator, Mapper, and Point Man) as needed or desired.

Designated Positions

As in baseball, there are some folks who are like idiot savants. They are good at one thing and one thing only. The other side of this coin, of course, is that they shouldn't be trusted with any other tasks. For example, what if everyone in the car has several points on their license, and one person has a perfect record? There's your Driver. Unbelievable pick-up potential? Some people just have "IT." There's your "First-in-the-door" at bars and clubs. These positions are completely flexible and depend entirely on the talents of your crew.

Star Tripper

A rarity, this is a person who is eligible to be a Trip Mate by dint of being either rock star famous or someone who's really dim but really rich. They don't serve any tangible purpose at all. Let's just be gracious and say this type of Tripper has something, well, "special" to give. And with any luck, they will serve as a major attraction at all the right times.

CHAPTER 9

ROAD TRIP ETIQUETTE
Or, "Do I Need Permission for This?"

The Road Trip is like a little country on wheels. A democracy, with the Driver as president, dictator, despot—it all depends what you let him get away with. Many things should come before a vote, all with the success and happiness of its citizenry in mind.

Nevertheless.

The happiness of the car's denizens is nothing to toy with, and, like government, its balance is delicate indeed. But in any society there must be laws to preserve peace and prevent total mayhem. To that end, here are some guidelines that work pretty well, though your car and your Trip will undoubtedly have its own personality. Until you find out what this is, try these on for size. Etiquette and good manners go a long, long way.

> " *Let us go singing as far as we go: the road will be less tedious.* "
>
> —VIRGIL

Permission Required

As for the following in-car escapades, you certainly do need to ask permission.

Singing

There's singing . . . and there's singing *along*. Few will be given permission to sing and hardly ever *asked* to sing unless your Road Trip is on Dolly Parton's tour bus. In general is it permissible to sing along to the music that is being enjoyed in your vehicle, unless you are asked to cease and desist by a majority of the Trippers.

Reading Aloud

I mean, who do you think you are, Maya Angelou?? With the obvious exception of the Mapper, who may read aloud for navigational purposes, here is what the extent of reading aloud should be:

1. "Look, that sign says 'Free wings during Happy Hour!'"
2. Frequent readings, instructions, and updates from THE LITTLE ROAD TRIP HANDBOOK.

And that's it. And, of course, if you find yourself in circumstances surrounded by fear, say a silent prayer.

Playing Road Games

There are plenty of Road Games—even some mean-spirited ones!—elsewhere in this book, and they're all designed so that everyone in the car can play together nicely.

But then, the lurking undercurrent—the unsupervised games: Chicken, Chinese Fire Alarm, Drag Racing, Leave the Loser (a popular laugh-getter played on someone peeing off-road), Speeding-Out-of-Control, and so on. These games are generally considered ethical conundrums, with a "someone's going to end up in tears" theme. The very key to each of these games' enjoyment is that *one person must die*. Otherwise, what's the fun? So, look into your hearts before someone gets hurt.

KENTUCKY's *Thunder over Louisville, the nation's largest annual fireworks display, is the highlight of Derby Week every May.*

Unshared Supplies

Oh sure, you have a right to your own potato chips and dip and foie gras and devil dogs and breath mints, and even nonedible items like hairbrushes and underpants and condoms and extra cash, but at the crux of the Road Trip is the ability to get along. So c'mon. Praise the Lord and pass the Doritos.

Oh, and if one Tripper is being especially piggy, ganging up is absolutely OK.

Unshared Substances

Oooh, I wouldn't if I were you. That's an accident waiting to happen.

Smoking

At this point, the world seems unclear as to what's worse to smoke—the legal or the illegal stuff. The latter probably deserves a private conversation among yourselves, but for the (still) legal stuff: of course, a smokers-only car, though rare these days, is what freedom's all about.

You and your buddies will need to make a set of sub-rules about open windows, outside temperature, chain-smoking, etc. Just remember, you may well be jeopardizing your chances later on, when there's a full moon and  romance beckons, if you know what I mean. Given the way you and your vehicle smell. I'm just sayin'.

Rear-Speaker Volume

This is the lone exception to the infallible music rule, in which that the Driver is king of all music. Back-seaters may discuss among themselves the option for rear-speaker silence while riding in the rear, and request same. This exception is designed to facilitate integral verbal communication with the front-seat Trippers, the Driver and Navigator, including, but not limited to, ogling, game-playing, and decisions regarding food and drink.

Snoring

There is no permission for snoring. No girlish purr, no temporary license, no excuses, no exceptions. No snoring. No kidding.

ZZZZZZZZZ zzzzzzzzzzzzzzzzzzzzzzzzz

Pit Stops

Though it's easy to lose patience with a car full of requests to stop for needs both psychological and physical, you'll do well to remember that soon enough, it's going to be you asking. Before leaving, decide among yourselves an approximate, yet regular, break schedule. Two hours, the usual time calculated for each job, or "watch," though it might seem short, is a good rule of thumb. The driver doesn't get too tired, and the rest of you Trippers don't get too tired of the Driver (and, it goes without saying, his or her musical choices). Everyone moves clockwise a position, and the clever Mapper will have picked out a happy and appropriate pit stop.

Exceptions:

Shopping Stops: Sometimes a little something just cries out to be fondled and tried on for size . . . something without two legs, that is.

Flashing Neon: Like a circus sideshow, it can just pull you in.

Avoid the ones which offer religious salvation.

Bathroom-Related: You can tell when someone really, really means it.

Use of a Personal Music Player (CD or MP3)

As the source of a musical library for the delight of your Trip, it's very nearly a necessity; for use with headphones, absolutely outlawed. The Road Trip is a religious experience to be shared among friends. Save your loner act for your living room.

" *The journey is the reward.* "
—TAO SAYING

Seat Adjustment

Do not mistake giving a warning as receiving permission in this delicate matter. As on a ship, any navigation should be announced and acknowledged. One does not want to hear "Movin' my seat!" answered with "Ow! You @#!&*!"

Within reason, the Driver needs what she needs as far as leg room is concerned, though, as in most matters, good manners are the guide. But the other front-seat passenger, the Navigator, must adhere to a specific mathematical equation:

$$\text{Knees } X + 4$$

This means the Tripper behind the seat being moved needs enough leg room to be able to cross his legs ("X"), plus have an additional 4 inches between his knee and the seat in front of him. This will comfortably allow for leg crossing and recrossing, map reading, and snack-tray preparation.

Cell Phone Use

How annoying is it to be Road Tripping with people who are on the phone with someone else? If they're so great, why aren't you with them? Why don't you marry them if you like them so much? What's the point of going at all?

Calls should be limited to information giving and gathering and should be kept under five minutes, if possible.

> *Exception:* The Feel Bad Call, whose sole purpose is the exact opposite of a "group hug." It's a joint call from everyone in the car to someone just to make them feel crappy about not being on the Road Trip with you.

Open Containers . . . and Such

Now to you, illegal may be just a state of mind, and some would say that standing up to The Man is what made America the great nation it is today. But it's always sort of a good idea to have a discussion about what's OK with everybody, hijinx-wise, and what's not. The Man also has a reputation for being less celebratory than the rest of us. DWI is serious and can result in grievous injury and death to you and your fellow Trippers and to others. So, chill, and save the attitude adjustment for when you're off the road for the day.

No Permission Required

No need to ask permission for:

LOUISIANA's Battle of New Orleans, which made a hero of future president Andrew Jackson, was fought two weeks after the War of 1812 was already over.

Sleeping

Back-seat Trippers only. The Navigator must tend to the Driver's every need, including slapping her around a little if she begins to nod off. But don't forget the "No Snoring" rule!

Breathing

With mouth closed only. Mouth-breathers are not welcome in the car, awake or asleep.

Road Reading

This is different than "Reading Aloud," above. Quiet consultation of maps and guidebooks is always a plus if it furthers the joy and "purpose" of the Road Trip.

Silent Prayer

Always encouraged for a safe journey. Silence allows room for religious differences. And who wants to talk about religion? However, many a previously agnostic Road Tripper professes they've gotten out of a car at the end of a particularly remarkable Trip, gazed heavenward, and whispered "Thank you, Jesus."

Wrangling Away Keys from the Driver in a Sticky Situation

Life and harmonic convergence being what they are, sometimes the designated driver turns out not to be the Driver "on call." That is, occasionally a person gets overexcited or overserved, and it suddenly might look like a good idea for someone else to drive. Make a pact from the start: if it looks too high and acts too high, it probably is too high. Anyone else who is less so should take over. If no one is in shape, go to a motel. Live to see another Road Trip.

CHAPTER 10

THE FREQUENT TRIPPING REWARD POINTS PROGRAM

Build Up Points on Your Trip and Win Extra Prizes

A top-notch Road Trip should reward its members the way travel and credit card merchants reward theirs. In the case of the Road Trip, the point reward system is reserved for good deeds and behavior above and beyond the Road Trip rules. You'll find that the more generous a Tripping pal you are, and the more often you hit the Road, the sooner you'll collect.

A Tripper receives 1 to 5 points for good deeds and heading off trouble.

MAINE *receives the first rays of the morning sun in Eastport, the easternmost town in the U.S.*

Because the program is behaviorally based, you should expect that some Trippers will do better than others. Here is a list of popular ways in which Trippers often make points, with attendant point value:

Remembering name of last stop, where someone left something - 1
Lending clothes, makeup, etc. - 1
Buying a round - 1
Getting free round from bartender - 1
Performing as food taster at sketchy food joints - 1

Entertaining the loser best friend of a major babe met on the road (Wing Man role) - 2 points per hour

Calling in an excuse for a fellow Tripper - 2

Lying in person for a fellow Tripper - 2

Changing a tire - 3

Talking police out of ticket - 3

Cleaning out car - 3

Making an introduction where a fellow Tripper benefits - 4

Cleaning out car after a "mishap" - 4

Serving as undesignated Driver in a pinch - 4

Waking up Driver (while at wheel) - 5

Giving up musical choice to others, even though you are presently acting as Driver - 5

Exchanging sexual favors with legal authorities for "the good of the Trip" - 5

Lost & Found Is a Great Way to Earn Points!

Listed here are some items that tend to mysteriously disappear on a Road Trip. Find 'em and rack up the points!

Finding Lost Things*

A pal's drink - 1

Free drink tickets - 1 point per ticket

Sunglasses, shoes, hat - 1

Prescription sunglasses, underwear - 2

Important map, address, - 2

Phone number from last night - 2

Corkscrew/bottle opener - 2

Wallet - 3

Someone else's money on ground - 1 point per every $10

Date - 3

Fellow Tripper - 4

Illegal substance - 4

Car keys – 5

Points for lost items are given only after standard 15-minute hunting time.

> " *[Travel seems] not just a way of having a good time, but something that every self-respecting citizen ought to undertake, like a high-fiber diet, say, or a deodorant.* "
>
> —JAN MORRIS

What passes for a "reward" is different for every Road Trip. A good rule of thumb is to give a reward to the Tripper who has the most points at the end of the day. Devise your own system, but here are some we've found to be popular:

Skip one turn in Trip position of your choice
Get first dibs on major hottie at next stop
Free lunch
One free lie from any Tripper upon arrival home
One free hour of musical choice (5 reward points per hour)

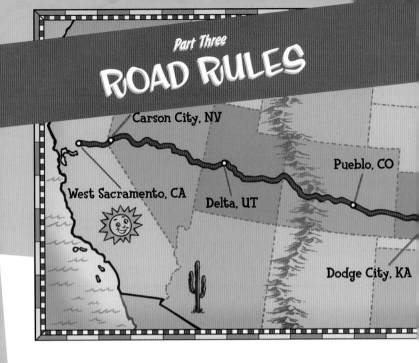

Carson City, NV

Pueblo, CO

West Sacramento, CA

Delta, UT

Dodge City, KA

CLASSIC ROAD TRIP #3–US 50: FROM SEA TO SHINING SEA

This is the ultimate test of Road Trip fortitude. Called "the Backbone of America" by *Time* magazine, 3,073-mile US 50 crosses the Continental Divide and wends through twelve states as well as our nation's glorious capital. But be prepared: this is no Las Vegas strip and is also known as "The Loneliest Road in America." But this lonely road *can* take you from sea to shining sea, which is its greatest appeal. Clever shopkeepers have kept the moniker alive by turning it into a marketing asset, and you'll find "Loneliest Road in America" passports, survival kits, T-shirts, hoodies, and other desirable souvenirs all along the way.

Route 50 starts in Ocean City, Maryland and ends in Sacramento, California. What states will you cross as you travel between the coasts? Well, beginning with Maryland, you'll enter the District of Columbia—which isn't a state at all, of course—then on into Virginia, West Virginia, Ohio, Indiana, and Illinois. From Illinois you'll cross the Mississippi River into Missouri, then drive through Kansas, Colorado, Utah, and Nevada before finally ending up in California. Besides our nation's glorious capital, you'll travel through several other great American cities including Cincinnati, St. Louis, Kansas City, and Carson City. As far as scenery goes, you'll see it all. Route 50 climbs mountains, spans rivers, and crosses lots of desert. It's a Road Trip that has it all, and there's nothing like going cross-country when you really want to get away!

CHAPTER 11

THE 10 COMMANDMENTS OF THE ROAD

Rules You Need to Follow Religiously

1. A Road Trip is the Supreme Panacea that cures all.
2. Thou shalt not put any other trips before it.
3. Love the Fellow Tripper as thyself. I mean, unless, of course, he demurs.
4. Honor thy Father and thy Mother by sparing them any details.
5. Thou shalt not kill a Road Tripper's story by blowing the punchline.
6. Thou shalt not comment on adultery.
7. Thou shalt not steal. But do work on comps and freebies.
8. Thou shalt, nay, *must*, bear false witness for another Tripper.
9. Thou shalt not covet anyone thy Fellow Tripper has designs on.
10. Thou shalt not covet thy Fellow Tripper's goods. Force him to share.

CHAPTER 12

EXPENSES

How to Pay as You Play

If there's one place money buys happiness—total, unadulterated, pleasure-seeking happiness—it is on the road. And yet, you'd hate for a few shekels to ruin a good time. I know, I know . . . you say it'll never happen, that you're all good friends, that nothing, especially a little bit of moolah, could get between you. And yet . . .

DETOUR

Show Me the Money!

If you're a college student, check out www.roadtripnation.com. You can actually apply for a grant for your Road Trip! They give hundreds of dollars to Road Trippers "who have a strong interest in exploring the world, discovering new roads they didn't know existed, and who are passionate about sharing those observations and experiences with others." Money is awarded at journey's end when your journal appears on the website. (See the site for more information.)

So you need an expense log. Get a pint-sized notebook for the glove compartment and jot down everybody's name, the date, and the categories below. Personalize your Trip, adding your own categories. It's a good idea, if some of your Trippers are on a budget, to settle up at the end of the day, or first thing in the morning, so that spending doesn't get too one-sided and resentment piles up.

Expense Log

Gas
Food
Lodging
Sex
Attitude Adjustment Equipment
Rock & Roll
Women (or Men)
Song
Other Entertainment
Road Trip Miscellaneous Expenditures
Snacks
Tolls
Tickets (speeding, traffic,
    concert, etc.)
Bail
Divorce Fund
Unemployment Fund
Medical Expenses
Other

CHAPTER 13
TAKE IT TO THE LIMIT (BUT NO MORE!)
Nationwide Speed Limits

OK, NASCAR fans—hold on to your stick shift. These are the maximum posted speed limits, state by state, for all passenger vehicles (that's you).

Maximum Posted Speed Limits

STATE	RURAL INTER-STATES	URBAN INTER-STATES	OTHER LIMITED ACCESS ROADS	OTHER ROADS
Alabama	70	65	65	65
Alaska	65	55	65	55
Arizona	75	65	55	55
Arkansas	70; trucks: 65	55	60	55
California	70: trucks: 55	65; trucks: 55	70	65
Colorado	75	65	65	65
Connecticut	65	55	65	55
Delaware	65	55	65	55
District of Columbia	N/A	55	N/A	25
Florida	70	65	70	65
Georgia	70	65	65	65
Hawaii	60	50	45	45
Idaho	75; trucks: 65	75	65	65
Illinois	65; trucks: 55	55	65	55
Indiana	70; trucks: 65	55	60	55
Iowa	70	55	70	55
Kansas	70	70	70	65
Kentucky	65; 70 on specified segments of road	65	65	55
Louisiana	70	70	70	65

STATE	RURAL INTER-STATES	URBAN INTER-STATES	OTHER LIMITED ACCESS ROADS	OTHER ROADS
Maine	65	65	65	60
Maryland	65	65	65	55
Massachusetts	65	65	65	55
Michigan	70 (trucks: 60); <70 (trucks: 55)	65	70	55
Minnesota	70	65	65	55
Mississippi	70	70	70	65
Missouri	70	60	70	65
Montana	75; trucks: 65	65	day: 70; night: 65	day: 70; night: 65
Nebraska	75	65	65	60
Nevada	75	65	70	70
New Hampshire	65	65	55	55
New Jersey	65	55	65	55
New Mexico	75	75	65	55
New York	65	65	65	55
North Carolina	70	70	70	55
North Dakota	75	75	70	65
Ohio	65; trucks: 55; 65 on Ohio Turnpike	65	55	55
Oklahoma	75	70	70	70
Oregon	65; trucks: 55	55	55	55
Pennsylvania	65	55	65	55
Rhode Island	65	55	55	55
South Carolina	70	70	60	55
South Dakota	75	75	70	70
Tennessee	70	70	70	65
Texas	Cars: 75 day, 65 night; trucks: 70 day, 65 night	Day: 70; night: 65	Day: 75; night: 65	Day: 60; night: 15
Utah	75	65	75	65
Vermont	65	55	50	50
Virginia	65	65	65	55
Washington	70; trucks: 60	60	60	60
West Virginia	70	55	65	55
Wisconsin	65	65	65	55
Wyoming	75	60	65	65

Source: Information from the Insurance Institute for Highway Safety, Highway Loss Data Institute, August 2008.

CHAPTER 14

FOOLISH LAWS FROM THE 50 STATES

Crazy Local Legislation

Drunk Driving: The Not-So-Foolish Laws

The Road Trip and The Drink seem to go hand in hand, probably because they're just about the two most fun things. Here are a couple of things to remember when combining the two. Of course, the designated driver option is still the best way to go.

What the government calls ".08 BAC" (Blood Alcohol Concentration) is the legal intoxication level in all fifty states, the District of Columbia, and Puerto Rico. This usually computes to four drinks an hour on an empty stomach for a 170-pound male, and three for a 135-pound female. But what constitutes "a drink?" One ounce of hard liquor, a five-ounce glass of wine, or a twelve-ounce beer.

Of course, you can also get pulled over (and worse) for driving with an open container. The following seven states are the only ones where it is *not* illegal for you to drive with an open container of alcohol (provided the passengers are the only ones drinking): Arkansas, Connecticut, Delaware, Mississippi, Missouri, Virginia, and West Virginia. Local ordinances often vary. **The best rule of thumb is never to travel with an open container in the car.**

Oh sure, it's all a lot of fun and games until somebody gets arrested. And it might be a lot easier than you think. The tried and true Tripper knows enough not to run naked down Main Street or throw a beer at the sheriff, but in some states, it's a lot easier to get in trouble than you might think. Understand, it may well be that a lot of these laws (and they are *all* real!) may just have never been taken off the books, but if you want to be the one that tests the police in Trenton, New Jersey ("You may not throw a bad pickle on the street") or Wynona, Oklahoma ("Clothes may not be washed in bird baths"), don't say THE LITTLE ROAD TRIP HANDBOOK didn't warn you!

Alabama

- A driver cannot be blindfolded while operating a vehicle.
- Having an ice cream cone in one's back pocket is always forbidden.
- The wearing of masks in public is not permitted.
- Men may not spit in front of women.

Mobile Law

- Howling at women within the city limits is forbidden.

Alaska
Anchorage Law

- No one may tie their pet dog to the roof of a car.

Soldotna Law
- People may not allow "attractive nuisances" to exist.

Arizona
- Any misdemeanor committed while wearing a red mask is considered a felony.
- Manufacturing imitation cocaine is illegal.

Glendale Laws
- Cars may not be driven in reverse.

Arkansas
Fayetteville Law
- It is unlawful to "kill any living creature."

Little Rock Laws
- Flirtation between men and women on the streets of Little Rock may result in a thirty-day jail term.
- No one may "suddenly start or stop" their car at a fast-food drive-in restaurant.

California
- Shooting at any kind of game from a moving vehicle is a misdemeanor, unless the target is a whale.
- Women may not drive in a housecoat.

Arcadia Law
- Peacocks have the right-of-way to cross any street, including driveways.

Cathedral City Law
- Sleeping in a parked vehicle is prohibited.

MARYLAND's sailing city, Annapolis, was our nation's capital from 1783 to 1784.

Eureka Law
- People may not sleep on a road.

Fresno Laws
- Selling gasoline to a drunken person is forbidden.
- No one may annoy a lizard in a city park.

Glendale Law
- Jump into a passing car is against the law.

Los Angeles Laws
- Crying on the witness stand is illegal.
- Zoot suits are prohibited.

San Francisco Law
- Wiping one's car with used underwear is illegal.

Temecula Law
- Ducks always have the right-of-way to cross Rancho California St.

Colorado
Arvada Law
- There must be enough lighting in establishm
  alcohol so that people can read text.

Logan County Law
- A man cannot kiss a woman while she is asleep.

Connecticut
Devon Law
- Walking backward after
  sunset is illegal.

Hartford Law
- You may not educate dogs.

Delaware
Fenwick Island Laws
- Laying down on the beach at night is forbidden.
- People may not change clothes in their car.
- No one can have a picnic on a highway.

Rehoboth Beach Law
- Nightclubs cannot serve alcohol if dancing is simultaneously
  occurring on the premises.

District of Columbia
- Unless sex is performed in the missionary position, it is
  illegal.

~~Florida~~ .da

- If an elephant is left tied to a parking meter, the parking fee has to be paid just as it would for a vehicle.
- Singing in a public place while attired in a swimsuit is illegal.

Georgia

Athens-Clarke County Law

- Making a disturbing sound at a fair is against the law.

MASSACHUSETTS'
signs along the turnpike marking mileage to Boston are measured to the gold dome of the State House on Beacon Hill.

Atlanta Law

- One man may not be on another man's back.

Columbus Law

- No picnics in graveyards are allowed.

Quitman Law

- It is illegal for a chicken to cross the road.

Hawaii

- No one can place coins in his or her ears.

Idaho

Coeur d'Alene Law

- If a police officer approaches a vehicle and suspects that the occupants are engaging in sex, he must either honk, or flash his lights, and wait for three minutes before approaching the car.

Eagle Law
- People are not allowed to camp out on city sidewalks.

Illinois
- You must have at least a one-dollar bill on your person; if you do not, you may be arrested for vagrancy.

Chicago Law
- Giving a dog whiskey is against the law.

Indiana
- A liquor store cannot sell cold soft drinks or milk.
- Passing a horse on the street is forbidden.

Gary Law
- Within four hours of eating garlic, a person may not enter a movie house, theater, or ride a public streetcar.

Iowa
- No kisses may last longer than five minutes.

Mount Vernon Law
- No one may pick flowers from a city park.

Kansas

- Pedestrians crossing the highways at night must wear taillights.
- Fish may not be caught with one's bare hands.

Derby Laws

- "Screeching" one's tires while driving is not permitted.
- It is against the law to ride an animal down a road.

Russell Law

- Musical car horns are forbidden.

Salina Law

- No one can leave one's car running when it is unattended.

Topeka Laws

- Snowball fights are illegal.
- It is against the law to drive one's car through a parade.
- No one may sing the alphabet on the streets at night.

Kentucky

- Throwing eggs at a public speaker is forbidden; the penalty could be up to one year in prison.

Lexington Law

- By law, anyone who has been drinking is "sober" until he or she "cannot hold onto the ground."

Louisiana

- Rituals that involve the ingestion of blood, urine, or fecal matter are not allowed.
- Stealing an alligator is forbidden; violators of the law may receive up to ten years in jail.

New Orleans Law

- Practicing voodoo in the city limits is against the law.

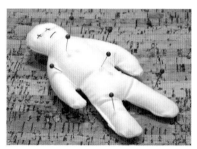

Maine
Portland Law

- People walking down the street must have their shoelaces tied.

Wells Law

- No one is to feed the deer.

Maryland
Ocean City Law

- Eating while swimming in the ocean is prohibited.

Rockville Laws

- Swearing while on the highway is forbidden.
- Citizens may not swim in the public fountains within the city limits.

Massachusetts

Boston Laws

- In case bears are present, no one may cross the Boston Common without carrying a shotgun.
- If the governor is present, duels to the death are permitted on the Common on Sundays.

MICHIGAN *is the patron state of the Road Trip, having long been the center of America's automobile industry. One of its finest moments? The 1939 Packard, featuring air-conditioning.*

Burlington Law

- Walking around with a "drink" is strictly forbidden.

Marlboro Laws

- It is against the law to buy, sell, or possess a squirt gun.
- No one may detonate a nuclear device in the city.

Milford Law

- No peeping in the windows of automobiles!

Michigan

- Any person over the age of twelve may have a license for a hand-gun as long as he or she has not been convicted of a felony.
- Seduction or corruption of an unmarried girl can result in a prison term of up to five years.
- No selling of cars on Sunday.

Kalamazoo Law

- Serenading your girlfriend is illegal.

Soo Law
- It is against the law to smoke while in bed.

Minnesota
- All men driving motorcycles must wear shirts.

Minneapolis Law
- No red cars may drive down Lake Street.

St. Cloud Law
- No eating of hamburgers on Sundays.

Mississippi
- Vagrancy is punishable by either thirty days in prison or a $250 fine.
- It is unlawful for a man to seduce a woman by lying and claiming he will marry her.

Oxford Law
- Driving around the town square more than 100 times at once is illegal.

Missouri
Excelsior Springs Law
- Hard objects may not be thrown by hand.

Mole Law
- Frightening a baby is illegal.

Purdy Law
- Dancing is strictly prohibited.

University City Laws
- No one can ask anyone else to "watch over" one's parked car.
- Honking someone else's horn is prohibited.

> *Two roads diverged in a wood, and I—*
> *I took the one less traveled by,*
> *And that has made all the difference.*
> —ROBERT FROST

Montana
- No one can have a sheep in the cab of one's truck unless there is a chaperone present.

Billings Law
- Anyone who has a "pea shooter" in his or her possession risks having it be confiscated by the police.

Helena Law
- No item may be thrown across a street.

Whitehall Law
- Operating a vehicle with ice picks attached to the wheels is illegal.

Nebraska

- Bar owners cannot sell beer unless they are also brewing a kettle of soup at the same time.

Nevada
Clark County Law

- Bringing a concealable firearm into the county is illegal unless it is registered with the Las Vegas Metropolitan Police Department. But, to register a handgun, it needs to be brought in to the police station. You also may not register a gun on the weekends; the police, however, may prosecute you at that time.

Nyala Law

- A man is forbidden from buying drinks for more than three people other than himself at any one period during the day.

Reno Law

- Lying down on the sidewalk is illegal.

New Hampshire

- Tapping your feet, nodding your head, or in any way keeping time to the music in a tavern, restaurant, or cafe is prohibited.
- Selling the clothes you are wearing to pay off a gambling debt is forbidden.
- Checking into a hotel under an assumed name is an offense.

MINNESOTA *is home to Bloomington's Mall of America. The size of seventy-eight football fields and home to more than five hundred stores, some consider it a Road Trip destination in itself.*

Claremont Law

- In cemeteries it is illegal for anyone under the age of ten to enter at night, get drunk, picnic, and enter by oneself.

New Jersey

- It is against the law to "frown" at a police officer.
- Slurping soup is forbidden.
- It is illegal to delay or detain a homing pigeon.

Caldwell Law

- Dancing or wearing shorts while on a main avenue is not allowed.

Elizabeth Law

- A woman cannot walk down Broad Street on Sunday without wearing a petticoat.

Haddon Law

- No one may annoy anyone of the opposite sex.

Newark Law

- Selling ice cream after 6 p.m. is illegal unless the customer has a note from his doctor.

Trenton Law

- Throwing a bad pickle in the street is forbidden.

New Mexico
Deming Law

- No one can spit on the steps of the opera house.

Las Cruces Law

- Carrying a lunchbox down Main Street is not allowed.

New York

- Throwing a ball at someone's head for fun is illegal.

Carmel Law

- A man cannot go outside if he is wearing a jacket and pants that do not match.

North Carolina

- Singing off key is illegal.
- If an unmarried man and woman go to a hotel or motel and register themselves as married, then they are considered by state law to be legally married.

n Law
- No one can drive cars through city cemeteries for pleasure.

Zebulon Law
- No one may walk on top of the water tank of the city.

North Dakota
- Lying down and falling asleep with one's shoes on is against the law.

Fargo Law
- If someone is wearing a hat while dancing, or even wearing a hat to a function where dancing is taking place, he or she can be sent to jail.

Ohio
- Getting a fish drunk is unlawful.
- According to the Ohio driver's education manual, a driver must honk the horn whenever he or she passes another car.
- No one may be arrested on Sunday or on the Fourth of July.

Clinton Law
- Anyone who leans against a public building will be subject to fines.

Toledo Law
- It is against the law to throw a snake at another person.

Youngstown Law
- Running out of gas is not permitted.

Oklahoma
- Reading a comic book while operating a motor vehicle is illegal.
- Anyone who makes "ugly faces" at dogs may be fined, jailed, or both.

Clinton Law
- Molesting an automobile is illegal.

Schulter Law
- Women may not gamble in the nude, in lingerie, or while wearing a towel.

Wynona Law
- No washing of clothes in bird baths.

Oregon
- Testing of one's physical endurance while driving a car on a highway is prohibited.

Hood River Law
- Juggling without a license is strictly prohibited.

Klamath River Law

- No one can walk down a sidewalk and knock a snake's head off with a cane.

Salem Law

- Women are not allowed to wrestle in Salem.

Stanfield Law

- No more than two people may share a single drink.

Pennsylvania

- It is illegal to sleep on top of a refrigerator outdoors.
- Any motorist driving along a country road at night must stop every mile and send up a rocket signal, wait ten minutes for the road to be cleared of livestock, and continue.
- Ministers are forbidden from performing marriages when either the bride or groom is drunk.

Connellsville Law

- Pants may not be worn any lower than five inches below the waist.

Rhode Island

- Before passing a car on the left, one needs to make a loud noise.
- Impersonating a town sealer, auctioneer, corder of wood, or a fence-viewer is strictly forbidden. The penalty for an offense is a fine from $20 to $100.
- Ropes may not be strung across a highway.

South Carolina

- According to law, if a man promises to marry an unmarried woman, the marriage must take place.
- It is illegal to do a U-turn within 1,000 feet of an intersection.

Hilton Head Law

- Leaving a large amount of trash in one's vehicle is considered to be a nuisance.

Lancaster County Law

- Dancing in public in Lancaster is illegal.

Myrtle Beach Law

- No one may sleep on the beach at night.

South Dakota

- It is illegal to lie down and fall asleep in a cheese factory.

Tennessee

- Daring a child to purchase beer is against the law.
- It is unlawful to place tacks on a highway.
- No one can carry skunks into the state.

Bell Buckle Law

- Throwing bottles at a tree is prohibited.

Kimball Law

- Bar owners may not let patrons make loud, unusual noises.

Memphis Law

- It is unlawful to give any pie to fellow diners or take any unfinished pie home. All pie must be eaten on the premises.

Texas

- Taking more than three sips of beer at a time while standing is prohibited.
- Because it contains a formula for making beer at home, the entire *Encyclopedia Britannica* is banned in Texas.

Abilene Law

- Anywhere within the corporate limits of the city, idling or loitering for the purpose of flirting or mashing is strictly forbidden.

Borger Law

- No one can throw confetti, feather dusters, rubber balls, whips or quirts (riding crops), and explosive firecrackers of any kind.

Galveston Law

- Anyone who sits on a sidewalk may be fined up to $500.

Lubbock County Law

- It is unlawful to drive within an arm's length of alcohol—including alcohol in someone else's blood stream.

San Antonio Laws

- Urinating on the Alamo is prohibited.
- Both sexes cannot flirt or respond to flirtation using the eyes and/or hands.

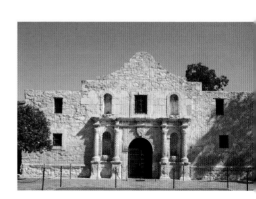

Utah

- It is unlawful to cause a catastrophe.
- Birds have the right-of-way on all highways.

Monroe Law

- Partners on a dance floor must be showing daylight between them.

Provo Law

- Throwing snowballs is not allowed; failure to comply will result in a $50 fine.

Vermont

- Denying the existence of God is illegal.
- Whistling underwater is not allowed.

Virginia

- No one can drive without wearing shoes.

Norfolk Law

- A man may face sixty days in jail for patting a woman's derriere.

Prince William County Law

- Parking a car on railroad tracks is forbidden.

Richmond Law
- Flipping a coin in a restaurant to see who pays for a coffee is illegal.

Virginia Beach Laws

- If you are drunk and not driving your car, and the person who is driving your car is drunk, you may both receive DUI's.
- Riding on the handlebars of a bike is unlawful.
- Driving by the same place on Atlantic Avenue within thirty minutes is not allowed.

Washington
Auburn Law
- No man can deflower a virgin, regardless of her age or marital status; the penalty is up to five years in jail.

Bremerton Law
- Shucking peanuts on the street is not allowed.

Seattle Laws
- Women who sit on men's laps on buses or trains must place a pillow between them; those that fail to do so face an automatic six-month jail term.
- No one can carry a concealed weapon that is over six feet long.

Spokane Law

- Kneeling on a pedestrian skywalk is forbidden.

Spokane County Law

- No stripper may come any closer than four feet to a customer.

MISSOURI's
Gateway Arch in St. Louis is deceiving: it is exactly as high as it is wide—630 feet.

West Virginia

- Making fun of someone who does not accept a challenge is illegal; the penalty for this offense is up to six months in jail.

Wisconsin

- Waving a burning torch in the air is a Class A misdemeanor.
- On public roads, livestock have the right-of-way.

Brookfield Law

- Tattooing is illegal unless it is done for medical purposes.

Hudson Law

- A person needs to have the expressed consent of the owner to sit on the owner's parked vehicle.

La Crosse Laws

- Playing checkers in public is illegal.
- You cannot "worry a squirrel."

St. Croix Law

- Women may not wear red in public.

Sun Prairie Law

- Hitting a vending machine that has "stolen" your change is prohibited.

" To travel hopefully is a better thing that to arrive. "
—ROBERT LOUIS STEVENSON

" If it is better to travel than arrive, it is because traveling is a constant arriving, while arrival that precludes further traveling is most easily attained by going to sleep or dying. "
—JOHN DEWEY

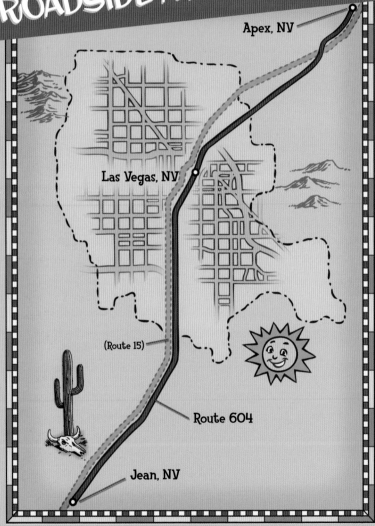

Apex, NV

Las Vegas, NV

(Route 15)

Route 604

Jean, NV

CLASSIC ROAD TRIP #4-NEVADA STATE ROUTE 604

In length, it's a snap to drive Route 604, but for some folks it can take several days and the contents of their wallets to make their way down it. "The Jewel of the Desert" is also known as Las Vegas Boulevard, culminating in The Strip, and it's truly something to see. And experience, of course. It's also probably the only road that's more breathtaking at night than it is in the daytime.

604 is only 37 $\frac{1}{2}$ miles long, but like the road to hell (paved with good intentions), or the road to drugs (a slippery slope), it is one from which some never return. It begins near Apex in the north, terminating in Jean, Nevada, on the southern end. As you travel north to south, it's like going into a time machine: you first pass buy some of the older casinos and strip clubs on the Boulevard, finally reaching the City of Las Vegas and the Strip, which technically starts at the Stratosphere and ends at Mandalay Bay, and the much-photographed "Welcome to Fabulous Las Vegas" sign. Whether it's the Yellow Brick Road for you, or the street where you lose all your green, it's not to be missed.

Chapter 15

"AS LONG AS WE'RE OUT..."

50 Nutty Side Trips Worth Your While

Now, you know there's no condoning "Destination Road Tripping." It can't be said enough: by definition, the Road Trip is carefree, without plan, reckless, even. There's no "We have to make it to Whoville by dark," or "Another 300 miles and we can take a lunch break." However, occasionally the Road can make you restless, and if there's no mischief around the corner, you may find you need to make your own.

———— **DETOUR** ————

Ask the Locals

From good food to hot spots to town traditions, it's always a good bet to chat up the waitresses, gas station owners, and man on the street for advice on what to hit—or miss. Also, keep your eye on the locals' behavior and manners so as to avoid being offensive. Getting run out of town is usually an unfortunate Road Trip experience

There are entire landscapes of devilment, of course: towns like Las Vegas and Key West come to mind. But for those times when you need a little soupçon of stupidity, here they are—one place per state that you can go, just to assure that both your mind and your journey remain delightfully off-course.

Alabama

Ave Maria Grotto
1600 St. Bernard Drive SE
Cullman, AL 35055
(256) 734-4110

This fabulous, bejeweled and bejunked array of 125 religious miniatures, such as the Shrine at Lourdes and famous buildings of the Holy Land, were the life-long hobby of Brother Joseph, who is buried on the grounds. They're all here (including a few nonreligious favorites like the Colosseum and the Tower of Pisa), and incredibly accurate.

Alaska

Santa Claus House
101 Saint Nicholas Drive
North Pole, AK 99705
(907) 488-2200

Ten miles north of Fairbanks is the mecca of children (of all ages, as they say) everywhere. It looks just like you always dreamed it would: Prancer, Comet, and Cupid nearby and available for photo ops, a gigantic Santa statue, and a fabulous Christmas gift store. Buy a "Letter from Santa" and even a piece of the North Pole. Very merry.

Arizona

The Shady Dell
1 Old Douglas Rd.
Bisbee, AZ 85603
(520) 432-3567

The Shady Dell has offered solace for the weary traveler in the most vintage of ways: fabulous old aluminum trailers, tricked out with retro furniture, black-and-white TVs, even old records. Add a visit to Dot's Diner, right on the premises, and it's a total trip back in time.

Arkansas

Christ of the Ozarks
Passion Play Rd.
Eureka Springs, AR 72632
(866) 566-3565

If every once in a while you still feel like God is watching you, you'll freak your freak when you check the horizon almost anywhere around funky little Eureka Springs. Standing tall at 250 feet, this statue of Jesus lords over the site of the Great Passion Play.

California

Salvation Mountain
East Beal Road
Niland, CA 92257

A crazy quilt of religious folk art (some might say obsession) painted on a man-made hill in the California desert. Artist Leonard

Knight lives onsite in the Salvation Truck, an ancient vehicle with a house on its back.

Colorado

"America, Why I Love Her"
Denver International Airport
8500 Pena Blvd.
Denver, CO 80249

One day artist and Continental Airlines customer service agent Gary Sweeney took all of his free miles and set out to visit more than two hundred weird and wacky places, where he took some nutty snapshots. This map of the U.S.A. is a paean to Road Tripping like no other.

Connecticut

The Barnum Museum
820 Main Street
Bridgeport, CT 06604
(203) 331-1104

The man who brought us "The Greatest Show on Earth" left behind a quirky museum filled with stuff like the Fejee Mermaid, a souvenir piece of cake from Tom Thumb's 1863 wedding, models of fantastic miniature circuses, and a 700-pound baby elephant.

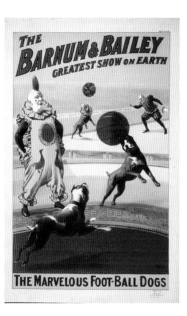

Delaware

Boardwalk at Rehoboth Beach
Rehoboth Beach, DE 19971

From Funland to stromboli to Whac-A-Mole to eye-popping people-watching, this is America in all its Road Tripness. It's a mile of too much of everything, and still you leave it wanting more.

MONTANA *is a state where you want to keep your eye on the road: it has the largest herd of migratory elk and the most trumpeter swans in the country.*

District of Columbia

National Museum of Health and Medicine
6900 Georgia Avenue NW
Washington, DC 20306
202-782-2200

Founded in 1862 to document the effects of war wounds and disease on the human body, it is one of the only museums in the United States that collects and displays human remains. You'll find more than 5,000 skeletal specimens, 10,000 preserved organs, and 12,000 medical objects. Among the many oddities you can see are a Cyclops baby, a two-headed baby, and a preserved Elephantitus testicle.

Florida

Weeki Wachee Springs Waterpark
6131 Commercial Way
Weeki Wachee, FL 34606
(352) 596-2062

The world-famous mermaids of Weeki Wachee have been swimming their way into peoples' hearts since 1947, and it is as offbeat a tourist magnet as ever. But these days you can also see "Pocahontas Meets the Little Mermaid," or even pose with a mermaid.

Georgia

The World of Coca-Cola
121 Baker St. NW
Atlanta, GA 30313-1807
(404) 676-5151

It's served over one billion times a day and is perhaps the biggest consumer product ever. Shouldn't you go and pay homage, perhaps buy a few trinkets?

Hawaii

Pineapple Garden Maze
Dole Plantation
64-1550 Kamehameha Hwy.
Wahiawa, HI 96786
(808) 621-8408

At 500 feet by 200 feet, it covers 100,000 square feet and is cited as the world's largest maze in the Guinness Book of World records. Sure it's easy to get lost in, but if you're in Hawaii, chances are you were already lost anyway.

Idaho

World Potato Exposition
Idaho Potato Museum
130 NW Main St.
Blackfoot, ID 83221
(800)-785-2517

Here in the Potato Capital of the World, you'll find the largest Styrofoam potato on Earth, the world's largest potato chip (25″ × 14″), and a wealth of potato facts—Thomas Jefferson introduced French Fries to the White House—and be able to sample some tasty 'tater treats, like potato fudge and potato ice cream.

NEVADA *is the second-largest producer of gold in the world, after South Africa*

Illinois

Super Museum
517 Market Street
Metropolis, IL 62960
(618) 524-5518

The only town in the U.S. with the name Metropolis is home to a museum which features part of the largest Superman collection in the universe. There are even two George Reeves costumes from the TV show—one in color, and a rare black-and-white version.

Indiana

World's Largest Ball of Paint
10696 N. 200 W.
Alexandria, IN 46001
(765) 724-4088

"If we build it, they will come," the Carmichael family believes. So since 1977, they've been busy painting this baseball every single day—so that it now sports more than 21,000 coats.

Iowa

Future Birthplace of Captain Kirk
Highway 218
Riverside, Iowa 52327

"Where the Trek Begins," the sign says as you enter town. Star Trek's Captain James T. Kirk will be born here on March 22, 2233. The "actual" spot is behind the barber shop.

Kansas

Garden of Eden
Kansas Ave. & Second St.
Lucas, KS 67648
(785) 525-6395

Nearly 100 years ago, upon his retirement, Samuel Dinsmoor began to build a concrete home and sculpture garden—and folks have been flocking to the Garden of Eden ever since. Adam and Eve are just the beginning: the Goddess of Liberty and the Crucifixion of Labor depict just a little of Dinsmoor's view of the modern ages.

Kentucky

Oscar Getz Museum of
  Whiskey History
114 N. Fifth Street
Bardstown, KY 40004
(502)348-2999

A moonshine still! Carrie
Nation's hatchet! Abraham
Lincoln's liquor license! The
history of bourbon's evolution!
Heaven!

Louisiana

Britney Spears Exhibit
Kentwood Museum
204 Avenue E
Kentwood, LA 70444
(985) 229-4656

What the world's been waiting for: the pop diva's platinum records,
Mickey Mouse Clubilia, and (gasp!) an almost perfect recreation
of Britney's childhood bedroom, frozen in time. And of course, a
gift shop.

Maine

Paul Bunyan Statue and Birthplace
519 Main St.
Bangor, ME 04401
(207) 947-0307

Folklore has it that it took five giant storks to deliver the giant of the forest, and that he was born in Bangor. This thirty-five-foot statue was donated to Bangor in 1959, on Bangor's 125th anniversary. Underneath the statue is a time capsule, slated to be opened in 2084.

Maryland

Final Resting Place of "Petey"
Aspin Hill Pet Cemetery
13630 Georgia Ave.
Silver Spring, MD 20086

At a grave marked "Jiggs" (though his real name, inexplicably, was General Grant) is allegedly the grave of "Our Gang's" favorite ring-eyed pup. Highly debatable and probably good for several miles of conversation. Wonder if he's the great-great-grandfather of Spot, the Target dog?

Massachusetts

World's Largest Thermometer Collection
Porter Thermometer Museum
49 Zarahemla Rd.
Onset, MA 02558
(508) 295-5504

Over 5,000 ways to tell if it's just you or if it really is hot in here.

Michigan

Mystery Spot
150 Martin Lake Rd.
St. Ignace, MI 49781
(906) 643-8322

Defying gravity. It's the real thing here. They're called magnetic vortexes or gravitational anomalies. It means things move uphill, people stand at the oddest angles. Extremely cool. Bring Dramamine.

Minnesota

Questionable Medical Devices Exhibit
Science Museum of Minnesota
120 W. Kellogg Blvd.
St. Paul, MN 55102 (651) 221-9444

From the G-H-R Electric Thermitis Dilator, or prostate warmer, to the McGregor Rejuvenator, which is guaranteed to reverse aging, here's everything you've never seen at your doctor's office.

WYOMING's *famous Yellowstone Park was the first national park in the world, named so by Congress in 1872.*

Mississippi

Mammy's Cupboard
551 Hwy. 61 N.
Natchez. MS 39120
(601) 445-8957

The last of the politically incorrect roadside attractions serves up the likes of blueberry lemonade and hummingbird cake for their luncheon-only crowd, with a little jelly and jam stand right inside Mammy's gigantic pink concrete skirt.

Missouri

The Elvis Is Alive Museum
Interstate 70, Exit 9199
Wright City, MO 63390
(636) 745-3145

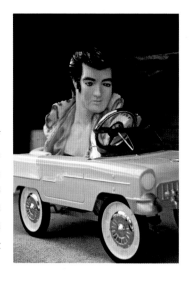

DNA test results, pathology reports, government documents, and more memorabilia are here, eager to convince you, as is Elvis authority Bill Beeny, that the King is alive. And while you're there, order a Hound Dog Hot Dog.

> " *No one traveling on a business trip would be missed if he failed to arrive.* "
> —THORSTEIN VEBLEN

Montana

Merry Widow Health Mine
Interstate 15, Exit 156
P.O. Box 129
Basin, MT 59631
(877) 225-3220

> RHODE ISLAND *issued the first speeding ticket in Newport in 1904.*

The thing that makes it impossible to sell your house allegedly also cures diabetes, lupus, arthritis, migraines, and all sorts of other ills. It's radon! Some say low enough dosages of radiation are the very thing for good health, so they come and sit and play cards and checkers inside this uranium mine, and others around the state. And if everyone looks like a Mennonite or Amish, don't worry: lots of them are.

NEW HAMPSHIRE's license plate motto, "Live Free or Die" is credited to General John Stark, a hero of the Revolutionary War's Battle of Bennington.

Nebraska
UFO Water Tower
I-80
Ogallala, NE 69153

If you see a spaceship coming toward you, don't dial 911—it's the local water tower, painted like a spaceship, complete with Martians peering out the windows, ready to abduct. It's also visible from US Highway 30. Postcards are also available in local shops.

Nevada
Nevada Shoe Tree
Route 50
Middlegate, NV 89406

There are shoe trees, and there are shoe trees. But many believe this cottonwood on "The Loneliest Highway in America," is the ultimate. Hundreds of soles are both hanging or strewn around the tree. Stop by and toss a pair for luck.

New Hampshire

Clark's Trading Post
110 US Rte. 3
N. Woodstock, NH 03251
(603) 745-8913

Just when you thought things should be more like when you were a kid, here comes a real trained bear show that's been bringing down the house since 1949. You can hardly miss it—the bears climb the signpost out front and practically flag you down.

New Jersey

Death Rock of Alexander Hamilton
Hamilton Ave.
Weehawken, NJ 07086

Where there's a duel, there's a dead guy—at least it's always that way in the movies. Here's the rock where the patriot Hamilton lay his dying head. Don't rub it for good luck; apparently his son died in a duel, too.

New Mexico

International UFO Museum and Research Center

114 N. Main St.
Roswell, NM 88201
(505) 625-9495

A dummy from the alien autopsy hoax, a gift shop with all things outer space, and a tour of the crash site? Out of this world!

New York

Woodstock Festival monument
West Shore and Hurd Rd.
Bethel, NY 12720

A paean to the greatest musical event of all time, on the original Yasgur's farm site.

North Carolina

Vollis Simpson's Whirligig Farm
Wiggins Mill Rd.
Lucama, NC 27851

Years of cast-off machine, bicycle, and appliance parts were scavenged to make this incredible spinning windmill display—truly junk into art.

North Dakota

Enchanted Highway
Exit 72 off I-94, 20 miles east of Dickerson, ND

If you thought that driving through North Dakota was going to be a barren wasteland, you're wrong: they've dedicated an entire road to fun. It is chock-a-block with the world's largest metal sculptures, spread out over thirty-two miles, from flying geese to Teddy Roosevelt to, well, go see for yourself.

> " *If you don't know where you are going, any road will take you there.* "
> —LEWIS CARROLL

Ohio

World's Shortest Street[*]
McKinley St.
Bellefontaine, OH 43311

It's fifteen feet long. That's it. Oh, Norman Vincent Peale and the Mills Brothers are from here. But not from McKinley Street.

Oklahoma

Ed Galloway's Totem Pole
    Park
Rte. 28A
Foyil, OK 74031
(918) 342-1127

NEW JERSEY and the New York Tribune offered the best promotional premium of all time when a lot in the community of Beachwood was given away with a subscription to the paper in 1914.

The centerpiece of the park's totem collection is the World's Largest Totem Pole, an amazing, complexly decorated ninety-foot concrete version built by original landowner Ed Galloway. Also on site is his eleven-sided "Fiddle House," home to his hand-carved fiddle collection.

Oregon

Funny Farm
64990 Deschutes Market Rd.
Bend, OR 97701
(541) 389-6391

*Or maybe just America's, depending on who you believe . . .

The "Off-Center of the Universe" is a bizarro world where you'll see the Dead Halloween Mask Burial Grounds; Bear, the hot dog-eating dog; an electric kaleidoscope that shows only "The Wizard of Oz"; the . . . well, you really need to see it all for yourself. Don't forget to pick up your bowling ball seeds on the way out.

Pennsylvania

Roadside America
P.O. Box 2
Shartlesville, PA 19554
I-78 at exit 23
(610)488-6241

It seems a contradiction in terms: the word's largest miniature village—a panorama of life in the rural United States.

Rhode Island

Green Animals Topiary Gardens
380 Cory's Lane
Portsmouth, RI 02871
(401) 847-1000

Camels, unicorns, bears, oh my!

South Carolina

South of the Border
I-95 US 301/501
Dillon, SC 29536
(843) 774-2411

It's a world of its own, and though we don't condone goals in the world of Road Trips, this is a destination that's actually worth getting in the car for. And it's the fireworks capital of the U.S. of A.

South Dakota

Corn Palace
603 N. Main St.
Mitchell, SD 57301
(605) 996-5031

Built and dismantled every year since 1892, this architectural oddity is completely decorated with corn inside and out. And speaking of inside: the interior features huge corn murals.

Tennessee

Graceland
3734 Elvis Presley Blvd.
Memphis, TN 38186
(901) 332-3322

What is there to say? Love him or not, Graceland is a national treasure. This is the ultimate tacky place to Road Trip to in the known world. Pack up your pink Cadillac, put on your blue suede shoes, and enjoy!

Texas

The Beer Can House
222 Malone St.
Houston, TX 77007
(713) 926-6368

John Milkovisch polished off over 39,000 cans of beer from 1968 until his death, and used every can to cover his house—not to mention surrounding walls, beer-can tab curtains, and more.

Utah

Hole N' the Rock
11037 South Highway 191
Moab, UT 84532
(435) 686-2250

NEW MEXICO *was the site of the first atomic bomb detonation in 1945 near Alamogordo; it was built in Los Alamos.*

A house carved into the side of a hill: 5,000 cubic feet, fourteen rooms, all the twelve-year pet project of Albert Christensen (buried right there with his wife, Gladys). Complete with a trading post, cafe, a two-story outhouse, a gigantic painting of the Sermon on the Mount, and a sculpture of FDR on this gigantic edifice, this place pretty much has it all.

Vermont

Ben & Jerry's Ice Cream Factory Tour
I-89 Exit 10 to Rte. 100 North
Waterbury, VT 05676
(866) BJ-TOURS

It's a tour! It's a "moovie!" It's a graveyard filled with the head-stones of some old ice cream favorites, like Bovinity Divinity and Peanut Butter & Jelly—all topped off with free samples. And then the astonishing news that every factory employee receives three free pints of ice cream a day. No fair!

Virginia

Lee Davis Texaco Station
Mechanicsville, VA

The Travel Channel calls it "the paragon of pit stops." Floral arrangements, candles, shell collections, and more are just the start. Because at some point on your Road Trip, you will do just about anything to find a clean bathroom. Reviewers everywhere say this is the place to, er . . . go.

Coningsby: **"** *There is nothing I should like to do so much as to travel.* **"**
The Stranger: **"** *You are traveling. Every moment is travel, if understood.* **"**
—BENJAMIN DISRAELI

Washington

The World's Largest Lava Lamp
410 E. Main St.
Soap Lake, WA 98851
(509) 246-1692

What would cheer up a tired town, a local art dealer wondered? The answer was as clear as day: the world's largest lava lamp! Formerly part of the Target store sign in Times Square, locals say it's the first lava in this part of Washington in fourteen million years.

West Virginia

Mummies of the Insane
Barber County Historical Museum
200 N. Main St.
Philippi, WV 26416
(304) 457-4846

Back in the 1880s, a farmer named Graham Hamrick invented a secret potion he was sure would mummify bodies as well as the Egyptians did. He contacted the county insane asylum for a couple of practice corpses, and as it turned out, the old coot had a pretty good idea of what he was doing. See the results here.

Wisconsin

Hamburger Hall of Fame
126 N. Main St.
P.O. Box 173
Seymour, WI 54165
(414) 833-9522

In 1885, Charlie Nagreen set up his hamburger stand at a county fair, and Americans have never looked back. Thousands of hamburger items are on display here, including the town's grille that cooked the world's largest burger—it took 13,000 people to eat it!

Wyoming

Home of the Jackalope
Center St.
Douglas, WY 82663

Sure, you've seen them in gift shops and tourist traps all over America, but this is the actual home of this make-pretend animal; in fact, it's Wyoming's Official Mythical Creature. The very first was made by a local taxidermist in 1939 and is so popular that the eight-foot tall statue that now reigns over downtown may be replaced by an even bigger "jackastatue." Also, jackalope hunting licenses are available (to those with an I.Q. of under 72).

" *My favorite thing is to go where I've never been.* "
—DIANE ARBUS

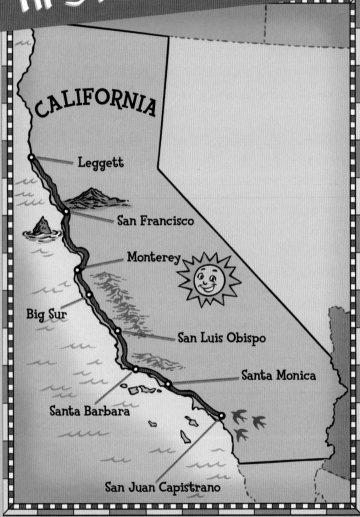

CALIFORNIA

Leggett

San Francisco

Monterey

Big Sur

San Luis Obispo

Santa Monica

Santa Barbara

San Juan Capistrano

CLASSIC ROAD TRIP #5-CALIFORNIA ROUTE 1: THE PACIFIC COAST HIGHWAY

At once so beautiful and so scary (sometimes the passenger side is so close to the ocean cliffs you can't believe you'll survive), this road is awesome in the truest sense of the word. Take it from San Francisco to LA and you'll understand what the pioneers were yearning for.

San Juan Capistrano in the south, through Malibu, baby, up past William Randolph Heart's San Simeon to Big Sur, the twelve-mile drive in Carmel, and up to the City on the Bay, San Francisco. After a ride through Golden Gate Park, Route 1 takes you over perhaps the most beautiful bridge in the world, the Golden Gate, into Marin County, continuing north until its terminus in Leggett, California, in Mendocino County. If nothing else, think of all the songs named after places on the Pacific Coast Highway!

CHAPTER 16

ROAD GAMES

A Few Ways to Pass the Time: From "On My Road Trip I Will Carry" to "Death Is Not an Option"

Now I don't for a minute think that you're so unimaginative you'll need to entertain yourselves with silly, childish games. But every once in a while a stupid game is the only thing that breaks up someone else's really, really, really, really boring story. Some of these are just sight or word games, but others may need to equip a Tripper with pencil and paper, which should always be kept in the glove compartment. And, of course, all games are suitable for wagering.

Death Is Not an Option

Imagine the two worst people you could ever end up with on a date—and making your best friend go home with one of them. The more players the merrier, as all the fun lies in the reaction.

THE RULES

Player One sets up the choice and poses it to Player Two, who must decide which of the two to have sex with, and "Death Is Not an Option." A choice has to be made. The trick, of course, is to make the choices as horrible as possible.

EXAMPLE

Player Two says, "OK, it's Amy Fisher or Heidi Fleiss. And death is not an option." And Player One must choose, amidst much laughter and discussion of penicillin. Or, say, "Howard Hughes or Howard Stern. And death is not an option." A nice dollop of extra difficulty is to make one or both of the choices someone who would not be of the player's usual sexual persuasion. Hilarity always ensues. And sometimes nausea.

In My Suitcase

This is simply a zestier version of what you remember from childhood. It's an alphabetical memory game where the players choose a bunch of stuff— twenty-six items from A to Z, specifically—to take on a Road Trip. As, uh, "grownups," the fun is in choosing your themes—hot blondes, things Martha Stewart would bring, or kinds of beer, for example.

THE RULES

Two or more players take turns "packing a suitcase," as it were, for the Road Trip. Every recitation must start with "I am going on a Road Trip, and in my suitcase I will carry . . . , " an item whose first letter is the next in play from A to Z. The player must then recite, backwards to A, all the items other players previously named to take on the Trip. When a player slips up and omits an item, she is out of the game.

An example of a sports-themed version playing from the letter G. "I am going on a Road Trip, and in my suitcase I will carry a Golf club, a Fencing epee, an English saddle, a Dart board, a Caddy, a Badminton birdie and an Archery quiver." The turn completed, the next player picks up by adding an "H" item to the suitcase.

Hint: The weirder and more obscure you make the item, the harder it is for the rest of the players to remember it.

Road Trip Treasure Hunt

Oh, the fascinating sights one sees on the road! The majesty, the ingenuity, the horror! Now there's a way to make some hay of these roadside "attractions." It should go unsaid that all of these Road Games require wagering, based on the likelihood of bagging the sightings. Here's a sample list to get you started:

- A swizzle stick you wouldn't show your mother
- Double entendre occupation bumper sticker, e.g., "Plumbers really clean your pipes."
- Matches from a strip joi—er, gentlemen's club
- Establishment offering lodging by the hour
- Girlie mud shields
- A car with antique plates

- A convertible with top down, windows up
- A parked car with a ticket
- A chauffeur
- A bike messenger
- A flat tire
- Driver alone, singing
- Driver alone, nose picking
- College window sticker from your own alma mater
- Roadkill bigger than a bread box
- Gay pride rainbow sticker
- Sexual escapade taking place in another car
- Crocheted or bejeweled tissue box on a vehicle's back shelf
- Car with equipment on racks for two different sports

Twenty Questions

Same as it ever was, this is just one great Trip Game. You don't need a pen or a crowd or a scoreboard or anything except what's left of your head from last night.

THE RULES

Two or more can play: one player comes up with a famous person's name, and everybody else tries to guess it. Each player gets to ask one yes or no question about the mystery person and may follow the attendant answer with a guess as to who it is.

Hint: Depending on how competitive your car's point system is, you can either give the winner one point per game, or one point each for the number of questions left in the game when the mystery person is unveiled.

Name the Bobble Head

Here's a new version of the license plate game we all played on family Road Trips as children, where you tried to spot cars from as many states as possible. What with the bobble head toy enjoying such a renaissance, the rear-end view of other cars on the road is still a great game site.

THE RULES
Set a time limit for players to "ogle for the bobble"—the Tripper who spots the most different bobble heads wins.

Hint: If you're in a particularly bobble-heavy area, trying upping the difficulty factor by limiting it to sports dolls, or celebrity or politicians versions.

The Ridiculous Restaurant Subtitle Game

"Good food and grog." "Your home away from home." "Where old friends meet." "Where the waitresses always put out."

What are these stupid promises? Who do I see about their not being fulfilled? I'll decide where my home away from home is, thank you very much. And what the hell is grog?

THE RULES

Obviously the gloves are off here for shouting out award-winning possibilities as you trundle down the lonesome highway. So one Tripper needs to be recording them. Write down the landmarks and who spotted them for the day, and vote when you pull into that roadside tavern at the end of the day. Seems to me everyone should buy the day's winner a round.

And speaking of roadside . . .

Road Signs

Try this list for starters—a point each for the Tripper who first spies each of these words on a sign:

Pies

Ye

Olde

Shoppe

Girls! Girls! Girls!

Beach

Native corn

'N' (the correct contraction—two apostrophes—needed for credit)

Hut

Seaside

Mountain

Roadside

Tavern

Saloon

Bait

Unisex

Evangelical

Christmas

Apples

Cabins

Air-conditioned

CHAPTER 17

ON THE RADIO

Music the Old-Fashioned Way

Sometimes you just want a little slice of what's local. To that end, a few great stations, state-by-state.

All stations are FM frequency unless otherwise stated

ALTERNATIVE	COUNTRY	NOSTALGIA	ROCK	URBAN
		Alabama		
Birmingham	Mobile	Birmingham	Montgomery	Selma
WMMM 105.5	WKSJ 94.9	WODL 106.9	WBAM 98.9	WBLX 92.9
		Alaska		
Anchorage	Juneau	Ketchikan	Anchorage	Anchorage
KRUA 88.1	KTKU 105.1	KFMJ 99.9	KWHL 106.5	KFAT 92.9
		Arizona		
Scottsdale	Tucson	Tucson	Flagstaff	Phoenix
KWSS 106.7	KIIM 99.5	KWFM 92.9	KLOD 100.1	KKFR 98.3
		Arkansas		
Fayetteville	Ozark	Little Rock	Little Rock	Pine Bluff
KKEG 92.1	KDYN 96.7	KOLL 106.3	KKPT 94.1	KIPR 92.3
		California		
San Diego	Sacramento	San Francisco	Los Angeles	Los Angeles
KBZT 94.9	KNCI 105.1	KFRC 106.9	KLO 95.5	KHHT 92.3

ALTERNATIVE	COUNTRY	NOSTALGIA	ROCK	URBAN
		Colorado		
Boulder	Durango	Denver	Colorado Spgs.	Denver
KBCO 97.3	KRSJ 100.5	KOOL 105	KKFM 98.1	KQKS 107.5
		Connecticut		
Waterbury	Enfield	New London	Hartford	Hartford
WURH 104.1	WPKX 97.9	WKHL 100.9	WCCC 106.9	WZMX 93.7
		Delaware		
N/A	Lewes	Milford	Georgetown	N/A
—	WXIN 105.9	WNCL 101.3	WZBH 93.5	—
		Washington, D.C.		
N/A	WMZQ 98.7	WBIG 100.3	WWDC 101.1	WHUR 96.3
		Florida		
Key West	Tampa	Ft. Myers	Tallahassee	Miami
WIIS 107.1	WQYK 99.5	WOLZ 95.3	WGLF 104.1	WEDR 99.1
		Georgia		
Atlanta	Valdosta	Clarkville	Savannah	Atlanta
WNNX 99.7	WAAC 92.9	WMIE 103.9	WIXU 95.5	WVEE 103.3
		Hawaii		
Pearl City	Makawao	Aiea	Honolulu	Waipahu
KUCD 101.9	KDLX 94,3	KGMZ 107.9	KPOI 105.9	KDDB 102.7
		Idaho		
Sun Valley	Boise	Twin Falls	Boise	Boise
KSKI 103.7	KIZN 92.3	KLIX 96.5	KJOT 105.1	KZMG 93.1
		Illinois		
Chicago	Springfield	Peoria	Macomb	Chicago
WKQX 101.1	WFMB 104.5	WPBG 93.3	WJEQ 102.7	WBBM 96.3
		Indiana		
Indianapolis	Terre Haute	Elwood	Ft. Wayne	Charlestown
WRZX 103.3	WTHI 99.9	WURK 101.7	WFWI 92.3	WHHH 96.3

ALTERNATIVE	COUNTRY	NOSTALGIA	ROCK	URBAN
		Iowa		
Alta	Cedar Rapids	Des Moines	Iowa City	Des Moines
KBVU 97.5	KHAK 98.1	KIOA 93.3	KRNA 94.1	KJMC 89.3
		Kansas		
Kansas City	Kansas City	Abilene	Wichita	Andover
KRBZ 96.5	KFKF 94.1	KSAJ 98.5	KICT 95.1	KGDS 93.9
		Kentucky		
Lexington	Shelbyville	Benton	Bowling Green	Erlanger
WRFL 88.1	WTHQ 101.7	WCBL 99.1	WDNS 93.3	WIZF 100.9
		Louisiana		
Thibodaux	Bayou Vista	New Orleans	New Orleans	Bastrop
KNSU 91.5	KQKI 95.3	WTKL 95.7	WKBU 102.9	KJMG 97.3
		Maine		
Lewiston	Norway	Yarmouth	Portland	Sisco
WCYY 93.9	WOXO 92.7	WYAR 88.3	WBLM 102.9	WRED 95.9
		Maryland		
Graysonville	Cumberland	Baltimore	Bethesda	Morningside
WRNR 103.1	WROG 102.9	WQSR 102.7	WARW 94.7	WPGC 95.5
		Massachusetts		
Vineyard Haven	Boston	Lowell	S. Yarmouth	Boston
WMVY 92.7	WKLB 99.5	WOCN 103.9	WBCN 104.1	WJMN 94.5
		Michigan		
Grand Rapids	Grand Rapids	Traverse City	Marquette	Detroit
WORD 97.9	WBCT 93.7	WQKL 107.1	WUPX 91.5	WDTJ 105.9
		Minnesota		
St. Cloud	Blackduck	Duluth	Minn/St. Paul	Minneapolis
KVSC 88.1	WBJI 98.3	KLDJ 101.7	KXXR 93.7	KTTB 96.3

ALTERNATIVE	COUNTRY	NOSTALGIA	ROCK	URBAN
		Mississippi		
University	Vicksburg	Gulfport	Jackson	Long Beach
WUMS 92.1	WBBV 101.3	WGCM 102.3	WTYX 94.7	WJZD 94.5
		Missouri		
Columbia	Branson	Kansas City	Columbia	Kansas City
KBXR 102.3	KRZK 106.3	KCMO 94.9	KCMQ 96.7	KPRS 103.3
		Montana		
Bozeman	Kalispell	Great Falls	Billings	Missoula
KMMS 95.1	KDBR 106.3	KLFM 92.9	KRKX 94.4	KBGA 89.9
		Nebraska		
Wayne	Winnebago	Omaha	Hastings	Blair
KWSC 91.9	KSUX 105.7	KGOR 99.9	KROR 101.5	KBLR 97.3
		Nevada		
Pahrump	Carson City	Las Vegas	Las Vegas	Las Vegas
KXTE 107.5	KBUL 98.1	KOOL 93.1	KOMP 92.3	KCEP 88.1
		New Hampshire		
Peterborough	No. Conway	Henniker	Portsmouth	N/A
WFEX 92.1	WPKQ 103.7	WNNH 99.1	WHEB 100.3	—
		New Jersey		
Petersburg	Atlantic City	Avalon	Atlantic City	Canton
WJSE 102.7	WPUR 107.3	WWZK 94.3	WMGM 103.7	WJKS 101.7
		New Mexico		
Santa Fe	Las Cruces	Los Alamos	Gallup	Santa Fe
KBAC 104.1	KGRT 103.9	KABG 98.5	KXXI 92.7	KKSS 97.3
		New York		
Woodstock	Olean	New York	Albany	New York
WDST 100.1	WPIG 95.7	WCBS 101.1	WPYX 106.5	WBLS 107.5

ALTERNATIVE	COUNTRY	NOSTALGIA	ROCK	URBAN
		North Carolina		
Southport	Winston-Salem	Shelby	Waynesville	Durham
WSFM 107.5	WTZR 104.1	WWMG 96.1	WQNS 101.9	WFXC 107.1
		North Dakota		
Grand Forks	Mayville	Bismarck	Bismarck	N/A
KJKJ 107.5	KMAV 105.5	KACL 98.7	KSSS 101.5	—
		Ohio		
Berea	Cleveland	Cleveland	Columbus	Johnstown
WBWC 88.3	WGAR 99.5	WMJI 105.7	WLVQ 96.3	WVKO 103.1
		Oklahoma		
Pryor	Alva	Oklahoma City	Tulsa	Bixby
KMYZ 104.5	KNID 99.7	KOMA 92.5	KJSR 103.3	KJMM 105.3
		Oregon		
Lincoln City	Redmond	Eugene	Portland	Portland
KSND 95.1	KSJJ 102.9	KZEL 96.1	KUFO 101.1	KXJM 95.5
		Pennsylvania		
Harrisburg	Altoona	Pittsburgh	Philadelphia	Philadelphia
WXPH 88.1	WFGY 98.1	WWSW 94.5	WYSP 94.1	WDAS 105.3
		Rhode Island		
Providence	Hope Valley	Providence	Providence	Narrangansett
WELH 88.1	WJJF 1180 AM	WWBB 101.5	WHJY 94.1	WAKX 102.7
		South Carolina		
Columbia	Aiken	Abbeville	Myrtle Beach	Sumter
WARQ 93.5	WKXC 99.5	WZLA 92.9	WYAV 104.1	WWDM 101.3
		South Dakota		
Brookings	Rapid City	Aberdeen	Rapid City	N/A
KSDJ 90.7	KOUT 98.7	KQAA 94.9	KQRQ 92.3	—

ALTERNATIVE	COUNTRY	NOSTALGIA	ROCK	URBAN
		Tennessee		
Knoxville	Nashville	Jackson	Chattanooga	Memphis
WUTK 90.3	WSIX 97.9	WMXX 103.1	WSKZ 106.5	WHRK 97.1
		Texas		
Fort Worth	Paris	Clarksville	Dallas	San Antonio
KDGE 102.1	KOYN 93.9	KGAP 98.5	KZPS 92.5	KCJZ 106.7
		Utah		
Orem	Salt Lake City	Salt Lake City	Bountiful	Tooele
KENZ 107.5	KUBL 93.3	KGNT 103.9	KXRK 96.3	KUUU 92.1
		Vermont		
Manchester	Newport	Bennington	Brattleboro	N/A
WEQX 102.7	WIKE 1490 AM	WBTN 1370 AM	WKVT 92.7	—
		Virginia		
Chesapeake	Danville	Lynchburg	Norfolk	Norfolk
WKOC 93.7	WAKG 103.3	WZZU 97.9	WNOR 98.7	WOWI 102.9
		Washington		
Seattle	Wenatchee	Walla Walla	Yakima	Seattle
KRQI 96.5	KKRV 104.7	KNLT 95.7	KATS 94.5	KUBE 93.3
		West Virginia		
Dunbar	Huntington	Vienna	Wheeling	N/A
WZJO 94.5	WTCR 103.3	WDMX 100.1	WEGW 107.5	—
		Wisconsin		
Ripon	Whitewater	Peshtigo	Milwaukee	Racine
WRPN 90.1	WSLD 104.5	WSFQ 96.3	WLZR 102.9	WKKV 100.7
		Wyoming		
Jackson	Cheyenne	Cheyenne	Powell	Newcastle
KMTN 96.9	KOLZ 100.7	KRRR 104.9	KLZY 92.5	KRKI 99.5

CHAPTER 18
EXCUSES, EXCUSES!

Or, Never Say "I Should Have Said" Again, and a Plethora of Getaway Goodies for the Boss, Your Boyfriend, or Even Your Wife

When you speak of excuses to take an unscheduled vacation—and you will—it is truly a matter of different strokes for different folks. The whopper you might tell your boss is completely different than the fish tale you may weave for your boyfriend. And your wife . . . well, that's another story (and it had better be a good one) altogether.

So try some of these top-notch excuses on for size. Some might work for only a day, but it could be a day you really, really need.

For Your Boss

- The FBI came to your house to question you regarding some of the company's business practices. An incredulous "I thought you knew" is always a nice closer.
- Car trouble. After a while, it sometimes makes sense to cite trouble with other people's cars, too.

- Last-minute school interview/award ceremony/teacher's conference for your kids. If you've any foresight at all, you should spend some time concocting the lore of a troubled child at home.
- False arrest.
- Lost your electricity. The alarm didn't go off, couldn't open the garage door, etc.
- A tree fell on your car.
- My dog ate my neighbor.
- Surprise IRS audit.
- A bird/squirrel/raccoon/snake got into your house.

DETOUR

Road Trips with a *Raison D'Etre*

I just don't believe that a Road Trip has to have a reason. On the other hand, I am all for inventing a reason to get out on the highway. There seems to be a flurry of Road Tripping lately that's theme-based. The best I've heard is the one my pal Mary Beth took. She's still in college, so she had the whole summer to work with, and did she do it up right. She and her boyfriend designed their Trip according to a cross-country concert schedule. I've also heard recent tales about shopping tours, including the mother of all stops, the Mall of America in Minnesota. Great roller coasters, the best beaches, you name it.

But damn, I wish I'd done that concert route.

For Your Friends . . .

. . . who are nice enough people, but not really Road Trippers.

- Semi-annual work trip with your regional sales manager. You can see the benefits of this one; you've already set yourself up for next time!
- Out-of-town reality show audition. And when you come back, you can say you signed a confidentiality waiver.
- Intensive motivational group training.
- Cosmetic surgery (on some part of your anatomy where it would be impolite to ask to see results).
- Imply Mob-related incident that is too dangerous to speak of.
- A trip with your old _____ to visit his/her old _____.
- You lost your Blackberry.
- Mandatory community service.

For the Loved One You Left Behind

- Yearly garden club tour/lodge jamboree.
- Called to testify before a secret grand jury.
- Found a box of puppies (kittens, a small child) you had to rescue. And yes, after much ado, you did find a home for every one of them!
- Someone slipped drugs in your drink. Don't push it by saying you woke up without a kidney; someone's likely to check.
- Religious retreat. If you can convince your beloved you're really a Child of God, you can go on a couple of these a year.
- Sequestered jury duty.
- Early—and secret—birthday/Christmas/"just-because-you're-you" shopping spree. This does mean, though, that you can't forget to come back from the Road Trip without a

gift, and then really put out with the expensive presents later when the actual day arrives.

- Checked an unidentified family member into rehab. Never release the name of this fictional relative and this excuse can be used more often than a dead grandmother.

For Your Spouse and Children

- Alien abduction.
- Off-site work retreat.
- Kidnapped by a cult.
- A friend needed an emergency intervention.
- Caught in midst of high-speed car chase. "No, honey, I really couldn't call you on the cell phone at 115 miles per hour!"

- Was secretly looking at newer, bigger houses and wanted to surprise everyone.
  When questioned later, you can always say the big raise didn't come through.
- Remanded without bail.
- Fell asleep under hair dryer at beauty salon and got locked in overnight. More brawn than beauty? Got locked in at the gym.
- Sensitivity training weekend.

CHAPTER 19
WORST-CASE ROAD TRIP SCENARIOS

. . . and How to Solve Them

Do you really think the Boy Scouts just came up with this "Be Prepared" crap out of the blue? Don't you think they came up with that motto through experience—*bad* experience? Here is a group *designed to help each other in times of trouble,* and yet more than 100 years later, they're still saying "Be Prepared!" This is because they know whereof they speak. They know that bad things happen to Road Tripping people.

Below are some common solutions to seemingly unsolvable solutions. As in the rest of life, you live and learn. It's time well-spent on the Road if you all concoct conundrums for each other, and see what kind of quick thinking you may be capable of should things go terribly, terribly wrong. Think of it as a parlor game that may save your life.

So learn from the Scouts. If you can handle these commonplace, bad-ass situations with a little savvy, you may even earn yourself a Road Tripping badge.

NEW YORK *has an annual Munchkins Parade and a Yellow Brick Road in Chittenango, Wizard of Oz author L. Frank Baum's hometown.*

You Can't Get There from Here

Some of you might not know about gas stations. Back in the day, gas stations did all sorts of great things: they'd pump your gas, check your oil, and clean your windows—and that was before you even asked for help! They changed tires and spark plugs and sold no doughnuts or lottery tickets. *And* they offered free maps.

No more. But happily, computers offer terrific mapping help. If you're traveling in style, you may have a GPS system in your ride to show you the way. If not, your home computer can give you a great head start. Not only can you get run-of-the-mill information on U.S. highways and byways state by state, but you can ask your computer exactly how to get somewhere, mile by mile, turn by turn. It's not as fancy as a talking dashboard, but it's a far sight better than the map from the old ARCO station.

mapquest.com
freetrip.com
google.com/maps
yahoo.com/dd
msn.com/DirectionsFind
randmcnally.com
expedia.com/pub/agent

" *If an Ass goes a-traveling, he'll not come home a Horse.* "
—THOMAS FULLER

When Your Cover Is Blown

Q. Your wallet is stolen. A Good Samaritan finds it and calls your husband.

A. "That's great, honey! I'd better cancel all the credit cards, though. I mean, jeez, how'd that wallet end up in [your Road Trip location here], anyway?"

Q. You accidentally got left behind at the last stop. What to do?

A. Are you kidding here? This could be the best thing that ever happened to you. Road Trip 101, man: go with the flow!

Q. You give someone your business card (your first mistake), and they call you at work. Unfortunately, you work with your boyfriend.

A. Don't tell me you haven't used the stolen identity excuse yet.

Q. You end up appearing on TV or in the paper the day after that big meeting you called in "sick" for.

A. Blame Photoshop. It's about time somebody did.

Q. You get a terrible sunburn when you were supposedly throwing up all day.

A. Draw dots all over your face, consult a medical website for names of unusual diseases, and say you have to stick close to the phone as you're waiting to hear from the Center for Disease Control. And the funny thing about this disease? They say it may come back.

WASHINGTON *has the country's biggest ferry fleet, traveling to the islands of Puget Sound.*

Q. Despite your best efforts to put together a car full of folks who would have the time of their lives, a fight ensues. Now everyone's unhappy, and either someone's got to go or there needs to be a truce. How to fix it?

A. Money and sexual favors, what else?

Q. You don't quite remember everything about last night. What to do?

A. If you are foggy on the details, chances are everyone else is, too. Piece together the facts each of you can offer, devise a story, and make sure you all stick to it.

Q. You have been fingerprinted by the police. How do you explain the ink on your hands?

A. At work, you call it an interactive home art project. At home, you call it a Homeland Security request at work.

Q. You end up in the hospital.

A. Well, it's a car accident, isn't it? A ride home from work with a friend, a taxi driver, a last-minute offsite seminar if the hospital's out-of-town. If the only clothing with you is your bathing suit, you were dressed for a company skit. If you have no clothes at all, it was armed robbery by a homeless person. You get the gist; take it from here.

Q. You can't remember his/her name.

A. What makes you think he/she will remember yours? Count yourself lucky if you can recall your own.

Chapter 20

THE 10 CLASSIC ROAD TRIP CARS OF ALL TIME

Climb Behind the Wheel and Dream . . .

These ten cars below—in no particular order—are the ones, I feel, should be the driving stairway to heaven.

VW Bus	It's never too late to get back to the Garden.
VW Bug	Now's your chance to see if you can still get to third base in the back seat without a trip to the chiropractor.
Woody	The original '36-'37 Chevys, that is. Surf City, here we come.
T-Bird	1963, turquoise with removable hardtop (complete with porthole side windows). My Uncle Bill had one. He was a bachelor and a reporter. He was my Hugh Hefner.
Any real mother of a boat	The B-52's would suggest "a Chrysler that's as big as a whale." That should roll you right up to the Love Shack.
1957 Caddy	Big fins and all.
Mustang	I learned to drive on a 1967 navy blue with a white convertible top. Thanks, Mom.
Little Red Corvette	Preferably 1969, with that juicy red and white leather interior.
Winnebago or Airstream	Still the best thing to rent for a wedding Road Trip. You, not the bride and groom.
Austin Mini	Any Mini, old or new, gives a little European flavor to even the shortest of Trips.

CHAPTER 21

10 THINGS YOU SHOULD NEVER PAY FOR

Hors D'Oeuvres Are a Given: But Here Are Some Other Tricks of the Trade

1. *Newspapers and Magazines*—If you're that prissy about pre-owned literature, bring surgical gloves. Come to think of it, bring surgical gloves anyway (free on your next doctor's visit).

2. *Tampax*—The finer hotels (not that you're staying in them) always have them in the bathrooms. Even in the lobby.

3. *Condoms*—As in the above situation for ladies, you may find them in the better bathrooms of night clubs. Otherwise, suck in your gut, and walk into a gay-friendly store or bar; they're always in a basket at the cash register. Just make sure you have one—you may not want to make this same Road Trip again later. If you know what I mean.

4. *Water*—B.Y.O.B. is the rule. Bring Your Own Bottle and refill as needed. Water fountains preferable to restroom sinks. Water cooler the best.

5. *Other Beverages*—As often as possible, using either your

feminine wiles, superior masculine charm, or your sheer, steroid-enhanced size as your only currency.

6. *Hors D'Oeuvres*—A great Tripper knows that almost any time of day or night, the ubiquitous roadside tavern offers a plethora of culinary delights—free nachos, mixed nuts, and even Buffalo chicken wings, to name but a few.

7. *Club Cover Charge*—Try leaving something valuable, except your drivers' license, with the lug at the door, saying you'll only be a minute—just picking up your friend.

8. *Lodging*—This is the time to use all those bonus points you get on your credit cards on a night at a cheap motel. What were you saving them for? A trip to Paris?

9. *Jail and Bail*—Well, technically jail is free. It's getting out that'll cost you. Oddly, it's often the very people you haven't asked along on your Road Trip that may help you out on the bail front: parents, bosses, wives, attorneys.

10. *A Note on Games of Chance*—There's a school of thought which promotes the premise that "You have to give to get." In the world of gamesmanship, this is often the truth. And with a little luck, the getting is much more than the giving.

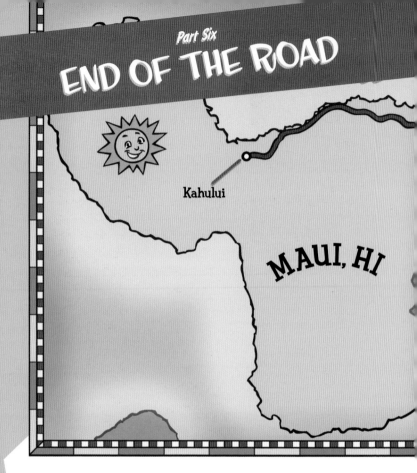

Part Six

END OF THE ROAD

Kahului

MAUI, HI

BONUS ROAD TRIP #6—HANA ROAD, HAWAII

Not to give short shrift to our sister states that are a little off the beaten path, a couple of Road Trip ideas for Hawaii and Alaska seemed to be the best way to end our Classic Road Trip suggestions.

Hana

Haleakala
National Park

Hawaii first . . . and the road trip gets *wet*!

As of 2007, the long-awaited Hawaii Superferry has made Road Tripping among the islands a breeze. It links Oahu with Maui and Kauai, holding nearly 900 passengers and 282 cars. Once on Maui, a Trip on Hana Road, the long and winding road that leads from the ocean toward Haleakala National Park, promises to take your breath away (it was a favorite of Mark Twain, Jack London, and Charles Lindbergh). At just over fifty-two miles long, the Hana Highway follows the old King's Trail, which had been the island's main path for decades. You go from 0 to 10,000 feet following switchbacks, crossing single lane bridges, passing crazy rubber-neckers, and with so many gorgeous places to stop, you could take all day. However, if you keep your wits about you can make it in two hours. It all ends at the ultimate overlook, Puu Ulaula, which is 10,023 feet above sea level and offers a 360-degree view of the other Hawaiian Islands: Hawaii, Lanai, Molokai, Oahu, and Kahoolawe. If you can drag yourself out of the sack, it's reported to be one of the greatest spots in the world to see the sunrise.

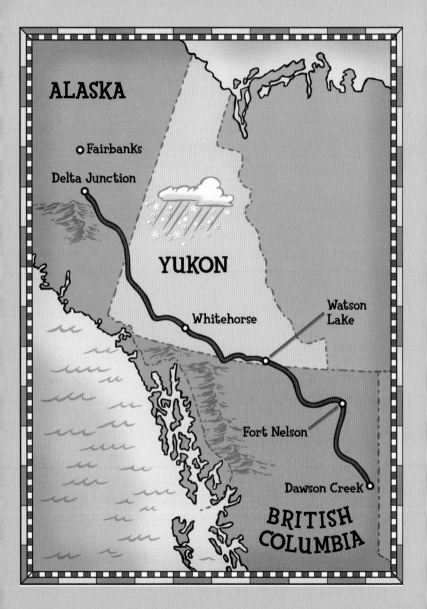

ALASKA

Fairbanks

Delta Junction

YUKON

Whitehorse

Watson Lake

Fort Nelson

Dawson Creek

BRITISH COLUMBIA

BONUS ROAD TRIP #7—THE ALASKA HIGHWAY, ALASKA

Mush! Welcome to the Alaska Highway! During World War II, while many of our troops were fighting around the globe, the Army Corps of Engineers were building a highway through Alaska. Originally it was primative—muddy, rutted, and twisted—but today the Alaskan portion is entirely paved.

The Alaska Highway (a.k.a. ALCAN or the Alaska-Canadian Highway) begins in Dawson's Creek, British Columbia, and passes through the Yukon Territory in Canada before actually entering Alaska. Keep in mind: this is no trip along the Hana Road. Driving from Dawson's Creek, British Columbia, to Delta Junction, Alaska—160 miles south of Fairbanks and ALCAN's official terminus—you'll travel across 1,488 miles of gorgeous road, including 201 miles entirely within the state of Alaska. (Watch your gas gauge: it's often 50 miles between gas stops, and in one place, 100 miles.) And if you want to double your pleasure, you can go off-road—really off-road—and catch one of Alaska's state ferries. You can do the Southeastern Alaska Inside Passage from the state capital of Juneau and other ports down to Bellingham, Washington, and Prince Rupert, B.C.

Cool fact about the Alaska Highway? It's the northernmost part of the Pan-American Highway, stretching (except for a fifty-four-mile gap through a rainforest) from Fairbanks, Alaska, to Ushuaia, Argentina, described by the Guinness Book of World Records as the world's longest motorable road at nearly 29,800 miles.

My friends, that is the Road Trip stuff of dreams.

CHAPTER 22

HOME AGAIN

How Sweet It Is!

You're back in "Kansas," learning, of course, that you always had the power to go home. With any luck, you'll now know a whole lot more. Maybe the revelation is that people back East—or out West—aren't anything like their stereotypes. Or maybe that they are. And maybe that's OK, too.

You learned how to talk your way out of trouble, and into good graces. You know the deep reward real friendship brings. You ate rattlesnake bits and drank your first Fribble. You conquered your fear of wide open spaces and put your trust in the hands of a stranger. You're somehow different, and yet closer to your true self than you've been in years.

—————————— DETOUR ——————————

Friends Along the Way

Making friends is what Road Trips are all about—that and T-shirts. It's a great idea to keep a Little Black Book of folks you plan to stop and see, or that you meet along the way. Old friends and new, and folks met upon the way—keep info on 'em all. You may want to ask some of them along on your *next* Road Trip!

You walk through your front door and notice that your living room is smaller than you thought it was. Maybe the paint is cracked in places you never noticed. The furniture is a little frayed. Maybe the yellow you painted the kitchen is even better than when you first picked it out; and wow, your home has it's own smell, just like everyone else's. How about that? It's foreign and familiar; it's all old and yet new, because somehow you are changed.

Night comes, and you lay your head on your very own pillow. Bliss. The hollow where your head last rested, is still waiting to cradle your weary, Road Tripped skull. Your bones, muscles, and sinews settle into the familiar curves and bumps of your mattress, and in those magical, always mysterious minutes where your conscious, rational brain, starts to give over to sleep, you glimpse

something. You wake yourself up to find out what it is; that vision—what could it be—so sweet, so deliriously desirable? That's right, Dorothy. It's the Road. The Open Road. And as you fall back to sleep, you start to think, to dream, and to *imagine* your very next Road Trip.

    " *No one realizes how beautiful it is to travel until he comes home and rests his head on his old, familiar pillow.* "
       —LIN YUTANG

Now it's time to take stock, and do a short, honest self-evaluation about your performance out on the Trip.

To wit, the *5 Questions*:

Are there moments of the Trip you know you'll always (want to) remember?

Are there parts of the Trip you can't recall at all?

Were there times you'd like to forget?

And are you lying there right now, on the one hand thinking, "Thank you, Jesus, for getting me home in one piece yet again. I promise I'll ne'er stray again"?

And yet, is there a tiny voice in the back of your head whispering, "Did I leave a six-pack in the trunk? Perhaps I'll just take a little spin in the a.m. and finish it off when I'm done driving"?

If you've said yes to all of the above, I offer both my congratulations and condolences: you're hooked.

ACKNOWLEDGMENTS

I never could have traveled up this highway to heaven without the driving assistance of some truly great Navigators: Steve Magnuson, Sterling's editor-in-chief, dear friend, and longtime traveling companion, and Ronni Stolzenberg, who helped keep me on course by doing some terrific back-seat driving. Additionally, my agents, Denise Marcil and Jennie Dunham, took the wheel when I needed them to. Sterling's bookmaking crew has always been able to cast my words into the most beautiful landscapes, and for this I thank Karen Nelson, Fritz Metsch, and Rachel Maloney. Of course, I owe special thanks to the Point Man extraordinaire, Scott Amerman. There will always be room in my car for these guys. It would not have been much of a trip without them.

And in the middle of writing THE LITTLE ROAD TRIP HANDBOOK, I enjoyed the most sublime and peaceful gift imaginable: being a writer-in-residence at the Writer's Colony at Dairy Hollow in Eureka Springs, Arkansas (which, by the way, is a great town to stop in if you're on the road). I offer my deepest thanks to everyone at Dairy Hollow for helping take me out of the workaday world to nestle in the world of writing.